FROM FISCHER'S SPECTACULAR SHUTOUTS

in the elimination matches; the selection of the championship games site; the demands, protests, apologies and outrageous psych strategy that preceded the match, to a concise and complete analysis of each nerve-racking game, including diagrams of all resigned positions and hypothetical alternatives to the moves that made chess history . . .

From biographies of the players to the complicated financial stakes of the match; on-the-spot coverage of the highlights, sidelights and fascinating behind-the-scenes activity; world opinion and reaction. Plus: how a novice learns to play chess; how championship contenders are chosen; the International Chess Federation regular rules; the special rules devised for the Fischer/Spassky games; and more . . .

For beginners, buffs and collectors—here is the most comprehensive account of

THE CHESS MATCH OF THE CENTURY!

A NEW YORK TIMES BOOK

FISCHER/SPASSKY

The New York Times REPORT ON THE CHESS MATCH OF THE CENTURY

by Richard Roberts
with Harold C. Schonberg,
Al Horowitz and Samuel Reshevsky

A NATIONAL GENERAL COMPANY

This book is available in a cloth edition
from Quadrangle Books, Inc., 330 Madison Avenue,
New York, N.Y. 10017

FISCHER/SPASSKY

A Bantam Book / published September 1972

2nd printing

Published simultaneously in the United States
and Canada

Bantam Books are published by Bantam Books, Inc., a National General company. Its trade-mark, consisting of the words "Bantam Books" and the portrayal of a bantam, is registered in the United States Patent Office and in other countries. Marca Registrada. Bantam Books, Inc., 666 Fifth Avenue, New York, N.Y. 10019.

PRINTED IN THE UNITED STATES OF AMERICA

Contents

Foreword/Iceland

The World Championship chess match has been held on an obscure island of which, before Mr. Fischer and Mr. Spassky put its name on the front pages of the world's newspapers, perhaps only four facts were generally known: some priests there a long time ago wrote some sagas, there are a lot of volcanoes, there is no darkness in summer and it rains all the time. Now for the first time in its thousand-year history Iceland is exciting curiosity beyond its own rocky shores. A look at the backdrop against which the champions played shows a land quite as extraordinary as the dramatic match just finished.

In the heart of the North Atlantic, almost on the Arctic Circle, the young island rises high and sudden from an empty plain of water. From a distance Iceland looks like a creation of the sea. Its ragged outline softened by snow could be unruly waves under a sky of storm clouds. Winds and rains of open ocean scour its dark peaks, and the snow of the chill Atlantic winter, swept from its rocky summits, lies deep in its cols and valleys.

Born of ocean as it appears, Iceland's roots are far below the ocean bottom. A fault of the earth, probably caused by the same cataclysmic force that split the continents apart some 200 million years ago, slices straight down the middle of the Atlantic Ocean from Arctic to Antarctic. This deep cleavage is a zone of permanent subterranean disturbance, the most continuously active volcanic area in the world. Out of its uneasy turbulence has been born the earth's longest mountain range, the Mid-Atlantic Ridge.

In the prehistoric past islands may have risen and sunk again along this line of violence, but since the beginning of recorded time most of the peaks of the 8,000-mile range have lain well below the surface of the sea. The only ones above water line are Tristan da

Cunha on the 37th parallel south, Ascension, near the Equator, the Azores, 39 degrees north, and far northern Iceland, a 40,000-square-mile expanse of crumpled, sharply angled land deeply scored by the elements.

It is a new country. When Cro-Magnon artists painted the caves of southern France, Iceland's 150 active volcanoes were still building an island out of a sea-washed waste of ancient basalt. While Judas Maccabeus fought and freed the Jews from the rule of Syria a mountain burst out of Iceland's northern desert, fully formed, in the period of one day. No one was there to see. The triumphs of man were being fully recorded in an old, already tired world, while unwitnessed miracles of nature wrought a new world out of fire, ice and water. It is still going on. Nine years ago an undersea volcano erupted and a new island broke the surface of the ocean like a sea monster waking, making Iceland .97 square miles bigger. Surtsey, an island of ash and lava, is the very beginning of the world all over again. The first eight green plants are flowering; the first few hundred flies are colonizing the hot sand; the first twelve pairs of fulmars have laid the first twelve eggs, one of which has been destroyed by a black-backed gull in perhaps the first murder.

Since the advent of man on earth Iceland has not been connected with any land. Though now technically part of Europe, her closest neighbor is actually Greenland, 190 miles to the west. Far out in the ocean beyond reach of primitive oars, sails or rafts, the island remained empty while over the rest of Europe civilizations grew and died. The Greek explorer Pytheas of Marseilles may have found it about 300 B.C. when he named Thule, the farthest land, where in summer, he noted, the nights were long and bright. A few Irish monks, in the seventh and eighth centuries, did find it. Seeking solitude over the sea away from the worldliness that beset even their quiet sanctuaries, they found in the stormy island the "desert in the ocean" for which they longed. A few settled temporarily on its south coast, where headlands of dark lava rear sharply out of the water and glaciers reach wrinkled fingers down into the very surf. They probably lived in caves along the shore, because they left small trace. When Norsemen came in the ninth century nothing remained of the adventurous hermits but some bells and holy books.

The Vikings came in search of booty and slaves, and they hit the ocean island by mistake, blown off course by North Atlantic gales. They found a fresh and empty land, its wide flowered coastal meadows untilled, its mountain flanks covered with a thick growth of birch forest. After looking in vain for people, farms, boats, on a shore that so clearly invited habitation, they returned to Norway with conflicting stories. There was nothing but ice, said one, who had climbed a hill and looked down on a fiord choked with spring drift ice brought by the Greenland Current. Not so, said another, the land was so rich that butter dropped from every blade of grass. The first speaker gave the island its name, his companion gave it its settlers.

Harald Fairhair, king of Norway in the second half of the ninth century, desired to be king in fact as well as in name. His nobles disagreed with his ambition, revolted against him and were defeated in the Battle of Hafrsfjord in 871. The victorious king then made the mistake of trying to convert them to useful citizens by taxing them. The outraged nobles, determined to remain proud, free and rich, emigrated in large numbers. Many of them went to the new island, this time to settle. They took their wives, their slaves, their cattle and sheep, their old gods, their high seat pillars—status symbols from their ancestral houses—and ravens to find land for them.

As each man debarked at the headland to which his ravens had led him, or the harbor where his high seat pillars, set afloat, had washed ashore, he planted a bit of earth he had brought from the temple of his favorite god at home, and sent a slave to run with a flaming torch around all the land he could encompass in a day. Within 60 years 20,000 settlers had thus established their wide domains, and all the usable land was claimed. The once-savage Norse raiders became in this brief space of time farmers, fishermen, legislators, patriarchs, founders of a proud new republic.

Their new land pleased them. A branch of the

Gulf Stream flows around Iceland's shores, softening a climate that in its latitude should be sub-Arctic. The settlers found tillable fields with thick grass to fatten untold generations of sheep and cattle. They found some timber for boats and plenty for fuel. They found ducks, geese, ptarmigan and sea birds in multitudes probably unequalled anywhere in the world, to supply them indefinitely with eggs, feathers and flesh. The meeting of cold currents from the Arctic Ocean and warm water from the South Atlantic, while it generated stormy seas and changeable weather, also created a climate of water kind to ocean life. The settlers had not only a bountiful land. They found in the waters around their country an inexhaustible fecundity of every kind of sea animal from shrimps to whales. A coastline of fiords made fishing easy and safe.

The country was not only prolific, it was beautiful. Beyond the green fields of the coast sharp peaks rose above white glacier ice. The birch forests carpeting the lower slopes smoothed the angular contours of the rocks and filled the air with aromatic sweetness. Hot springs stained volcanic hillsides pink and yellow and a strange muddy blue. Flowers of the north, small and brightly hued, made rainbows on the meadows. True rainbows arched from alp to fiord as oceanic clouds, caught by the hills, spilled their rain in sudden bursts through water-brightened sunshine. There were no stinging insects, no snakes, no predatory animals other than eagles, hawks and Arctic foxes. The sea-born weather gave the island an almost year-round springtime. Summers were not too hot nor winters too cold. In summer the sun shone almost all night long, while in the winter the aurora borealis played over a darkened snowy world.

The "desert in the ocean" sought by the Irish monks turned out to be, for Iceland's permanent settlers, a land of singular grace, peace and plenty.

The Norsemen built their long halls of stone and turf, the dark brown and gray of the mountains, cut into the hillsides for protection so that they looked like part of the land. Grass, moss and flowers grew on their sod roofs and the doors faced north to catch the full summer sun. They pastured their animals in the mountains while they reaped the season's two crops of hay. In winter they sailed the fiords with woolen nets and willow baskets to catch fish which they cured over peat fires. They lived comfortably, they ate well and they even had hot and cold running water from the hot springs that bubbled so surprisingly from even the most ordinary fields.

Each section of the country elected its representative, a wise man or strong paterfamilias, and these men gathered from all over the country to conduct a parliament which, over a thousand years later, still functions. Though Iceland was hardly a democracy and suffrage was something less than universal, no man among them had first place and all were equal under the law. In the Europe of those years, the feudal Dark Ages when abysmal poverty and ignorance went hand in hand with the blackest despotism, the young republic was a refreshing anomaly.

Iceland's first settler, Ingolf, followed his high seat pillars into the broad protected bay of Faxafloi and made land on a peninsula surrounded by mountains. He named his landfall Reykjavik—Smoky Bay—for the columns of white steam that he saw rising from the fields. Smoky Bay is probably the cleanest capital city on earth. The columns of steam come from underground hot springs, and they provide the city with all its heat. No factories dim the air with fumes or foul the ocean with waste. The extraordinary clarity of the air is the first impression a newcomer has. Even on a foggy day Reykjavik's many-colored houses shine as clear and bright as the flowers of the fields. Everything looks new. It is as if the city, and indeed the whole country, had come up out of the sea, clean-washed and fully formed, only this morning.

The reason for the remarkable absence of smog and grime is that Iceland has no heavy industry. A nation of farmers since its founding, the end of the last century saw Iceland change to a nation of fishermen. The country has no resources of minerals, chemicals, timber, any of the raw products on which an industrial economy must be based. So the industrial revolution passed her by. Having no industry, Iceland has no overconcentration of population, no slums, no unemployment, no mine-blighted areas, no crime (there is less than one murder a year) and—this is the pleasantest—no classes. The population is singularly homogeneous. Immigration has been almost unknown since the founding, and few Icelanders emigrate. They all know the names and histories of one another's ancestors. One cannot say, as in other democracies, "From the humblest farmer to . . ." because the farmer, not humble, is probably directly descended from Snorri, chief justice of the western fiords, son of Thorstein, son of Thorgrim, son of Thorolf who cast overboard his high seat pillars to found his new home at Breidafjord in the year 989. The telephone directories are alphabetically listed by first names, as there are no family names. Every man bears his given name and the name of his father, as does every woman. A married woman does not change her name; throughout her life she is the daughter of her father, not the wife of her husband. Their son in turn takes his father's name as his second name. Outsiders find this confusing but Icelanders know exactly who is who. Their history, kept green by the sagas of their ancestors, which all can still read, is very much alive to them.

Such easy familiarity could not exist in a crowded country. Iceland is about the size of Ohio, and its population in 1970 was 210,000, or about five people per square mile. The population of Cleveland, Ohio, in the same year was 750,879.

Only the edges of Iceland can be inhabited. The interior is a high wilderness of mountains and glaciers, the newest part of the island, where volcanoes are active even under ice. Vatnajökull, a glacier larger than all the glaciers of the Alps together, takes up 3,140 square miles of the south central section. Volcanoes beneath it still erupt, bursting through the ice and sending millions of tons of sand and rocks to obliterate well-known landmarks and change the shape of the southern coast. Its outlet glaciers touch the sea, and bits of them break off in storms. One finds these, blue-green transparent shells of old icebergs scoured into baroque shapes by the waves, washed up again on the black lava sands far from their parent glaciers.

Most of Iceland's rivers flow from Vatnajökull. Though it is a country where water is the most plentiful and the most noticeable element, none of the rivers is navigable. Coming from the heights they sluice through desert and pasture alike in rapids milky with glacial silt. Even on flat land cloud plumes spring out of the ground, and one has to be almost upon them before seeing the thundering waterfalls that generate the spume, falling hundreds of feet into spectacular gorges water-carved through multicolored volcanic work.

North of Vatnajökull is the vast central desert called Odadahraun—Burnt Land of Evil Men—a near empty waste of old and new lava fields. In the old days miscreants who escaped justice were said to have taken abode in the Odadahraun, but it is hard to know on what they subsisted. The plant and animal life is inconsiderable. Some hardy tundra plants show small leaves and bright flowers against the ashy ground, and sparse grass grows along river banks. There are a few areas where ptarmigan and golden plover nest, and the rare gyrfalcons hunt there, great gray shadows over the bleak plains. History records only two known human occupations of the Burnt Land. One is written in the Saga of Grettir, the story of an early hero of great courage and dangerous temper who, after one too many murders, was exiled and survived 20 years in the desert (he had friends). The second is the sojourn of our own astronauts, who trained there on ground strikingly similar to the surface of the moon.

To drive across it is not unlike, one supposes, driving over moon land. There is said to be a road but it is visible only in the shape of an occasional cairn. Enormous bubbles of lava congealed in wrinkles and potholes as they burst; long pale flats of aerated pumice, a rock lighter than water; surrealistic fields of ropy lava in twisted coils; floods of gigantic black cinders stained with thin yellow moss; distant volcanoes, their flanks rough with new lava, their icy peaks perpetually hung with clouds—nothing there seems of our familiar earth.

After the fierce desolation of the interior Iceland's coastal countryside is fresh and inviting. Tilled fields are deep green, edged with walls of the sharp red lava rocks that the farmers have painfully dislodged from them. Between the cultivated lands are rolling hummocky pastures with a thick growth of coarse grass, field flowers and willow shrub, where sheep graze. Wherever the hand of man is not, the sheep are, on heaths, on bogs, on the sheerest cliffs. In fact sheep have been largely responsible for the permanent denuding of Iceland. The low continuous birch forest that covered much of the land at the time of the settlement has disappeared. The early settlers cut it unmercifully, and when the new growth came sheep immediately grazed it to the roots. The result was that the soil became eroded to a point where trees could no longer grow at all. Some effort is being made at reforestation with suitable trees from Alaska, Norway and Siberia but so far it has had little effect. The result is a beautiful clarity of outline. The eye travels unendingly along the lines of headlands and ridges superimposed on one another into disappearing distance. The shape of the earth is clear and bold.

Even Iceland's attractive farmland shows only sporadic signs of life. One drives long on winding dirt roads that follow onetime pony trails, without seeing a house. There are signposts along the way, and a mile or two back from the road an occasional grove of carefully nurtured trees in a hollow marks the site of a farm, but the only clue to human presence is the roadside stand with milk pails on it. Cows whose heavy udders sweep the ground stare docilely. Sheep scurry off, their dense fleece bouncing. Once in a while a dog comes out of a lonesome field to bark and chase. But the people are elsewhere. The centers of civilization can be called towns only out of courtesy. Five or six farmhouses within a mile constitute a village, with a tin-roofed church and a gas pump to mark the town center. A small child inhabits the gas station, and one helps oneself to fuel.

Iceland has an extravagantly wrinkled coastline. As the last ice sheet retreated its glaciers gouged out innumerable fiords, bays and inlets, leaving the island with 3,700 miles of shore and an abundance of deep natural harbors. Here are the fishing villages, the bases of Iceland's economy, and here, at last, are the people. The towns are not crowded but they are lively. You see them from afar as you come around a stark headland or descend from an icy col: a cluster of concrete houses painted every imaginable shade—coral, cobalt, lavender, chocolate—grouped in esthetic coziness at the head of the fiord around a small forest of masts. The fishing boats vary from 40-foot lobster boats to hundred-ton trawlers, and they are always busy. The great catch is cod, but nearly every other northern fish is represented. The one ominous exception is herring. Until five years ago herring was the number two catch, with the seines often so heavy-laden that streams of fish had to be released as the fishermen drew the nets in. Continuous pursuit has reduced this useful fish to the point of no return. The herring no longer spawns in Icelandic waters, and Iceland's once large herring industry is dead. It is a prophetic failure. Over-fishing by modern trawlers with the efficiency of giant vacuum cleaners may spell the end of more than the herring. Iceland is the last great stronghold of the cod. Massachusetts is finished, the Bering Sea is finished, the Newfoundland Banks are going. The Icelandic fleet is not alone at fault. British, Russian, Japanese, all flock to Iceland's teeming fisheries. The ocean-isolated island, dependent on imports for every necessity, is faced with the possible extinction of its sole industry, the basis of its existence. The only remedy is to extend the fishery limit to a healthy fifty miles. This is not as easy as it should be. Iceland's suppliers, chiefly Great Britain, are threatening to cut her off, and the discussions are increasingly acrimonious.

The menacing cloud on Iceland's horizon has not yet begun to affect the spirits of her citizens. Generally they are a contented lot. They love their stormy island and do not want to live anywhere else. Why should they? Most of them are, if not rich, comfortable. Competition is not fierce, pressures are low, no one worries much about anything. There are no army, no navy and no air force, so they have never suffered the sorrows of war. Though they are proud and independent as their direct ancestors, one's first impression is of a sunny, relaxed people, kind to friends and strangers alike. On further acquaintance they turn out to be remarkably sophisticated, and as well educated as any people in the world. Literacy is 100 percent. In order to graduate from school, which he must in order to get a job, every Icelander has to speak two languages besides Icelandic. This is essential for a people whose everyday tongue is the ancient language of the sagas, not spoken anywhere else. The result is that they are well versed in the literature, arts, history and politics of the world outside.

Happily it remains the world outside. Icelanders are very much people of the twentieth century. But their home has not changed drastically in a thousand years. The mountains are as clean-lined, the fields as spacious, the air and water as pure as the Viking settlers found them. The lonely ocean island is perhaps a last outpost of an uncluttered civilization.

Katharine Scherman

August, 1972
New York, N. Y.

Katharine Scherman is presently writing a book on the land, the people, the flora and fauna, and the history of Iceland.

Introduction

The chess battle of the century didn't merely take place. It erupted. It burst upon the world's consciousness, and the flames that accompanied that eruption drew to themselves not just that small group of people who had always followed the fortunes of chess champions and would-be champions, but also the far, far, wider world of those to whom chess was a sometime, or even a no-time, thing, those to whom the names of the chessboard masters were total unknowns or, at best, vaguely remembered syllables with no images or meanings attached.

The world of chess—that small sideshow in the immense human circus—suddenly found itself moved into the main arena on almost equal billing with great political and social events. Millions were watching. Millions who had, perhaps, once learned the rudiments of the game but had then laid it aside; millions more who had never gone even that far. All were watching—enthralled.

At its highest level, chess could offer to its newfound audience, as it had always offered to its devotees, an experience akin in a way to that of listening to a Mozart symphony, for—at that rarified level—it is an artistic creation. There are themes and variations, subtle combinations, a dynamic range, brilliant codas.

Newspapers and magazines found themselves called upon to supply a rapidly expanding demand for news about chess. About the background of the coming battle. About the principal combatants and their retinues of seconds, assistants, helpers, advisers. About the site of the match. And, of course, about chess itself. The public's appetite for news about chess, for information about it, had been whetted. And much of that public knew little or nothing about the game.

There were books, of course; thousands upon thousands of them. Elementary books for the beginner, intermediate books, advanced books, technical books, general books, tournament books—books, books, books.

But for the vast majority of newcomers, those drawn to the flames of the eruption, those watching the performance in the main arena, those whose appetites had been newly whetted, newspapers were the main source of information.

One such newcomer to the chess scene was McCandlish Phillips, a reporter for *The New York Times,* who knew nothing about the game. Nothing. How better, then, to capture the problems faced by the novice than to send McCandlish Phillips to a master to learn. Phillips went, and dutifully recorded what happened. His story appeared on Friday, June 30, 1972. It went like this:

> To a man unfamiliar with chess, except that it seemed vaguely to suggest checkers gone berserk, the approaching world championship series, scheduled to begin in Iceland on Sunday, was rich with the promise of an adventure in total noncomprehension.
>
> In the weeks ahead there would be endless reams of chess news and analysis, much of it couched in incomprehensible jargon, accompanied by arcane diagrams.
>
> "Why don't you learn something about chess?" his boss had suggested. The uninitiate went straight to the dictionary. Chess was defined as "a game of pure skill played on a chessboard with chessmen . . . a game of ancient and obscure origin . . . probably imported into Europe in medieval times from the Orient."
>
> Having grasped as much of its origins as any man may know at a glance, he went next to the Marshall Chess Club, a cloister at 23 West 10th Street, where lovers and slaves of chess bend over the boards in hushed absorption, pursuing what is to some a game, to others an addiction.
>
> What scant pleasure the novice had taken in the prospect of learning about chess had been

shriveled the night before when a chess-playing friend had told him, "Chess is one of those games that, once you've learned how to play it, you know nothing."

Starting from a deficit position, it would be a steep climb to ground zero.

On the way to the club the novice recalled himself as the checkers idiot of Camp Frank A. Day, where he had worked summers in the long ago. "I had tots who could barely lace their own shoes, but they could always triple-jump me off the board," he said.

One thing was clear: If he could learn something about chess, anybody could.

At the top of the stairs in the town-house club, he met his tutor, Shelby Lyman, a chess master, a man of imposing stature, physically and intellectually, who gave up college teaching in sociology two years ago to devote full time to chess.

Mr. Lyman, born in Brooklyn, bred in Boston and cultivated at Harvard, has a foundation in psychology, anthropology and sociology, a solid bedrock from which to proceed to the higher art of chess.

To the Parcheesi *zhlub* who stood before him, Mr. Lyman came across as a modest and cordial man and William the Conqueror—a contradiction that made sense long before the session had ended.

It took less than four hours for Mr. Lyman to transform his visitor from a chess illiterate to a man with a certain ordered regard for chess.

From 1:15 to 5 P.M. there poured from Mr. Lyman's lips an almost unbroken stream of wonderfully knowledgeable talk, filled with erudite allusions that made the hours fly.

The novice had always seen chess through a thick haze of bafflement—it was as foreign to him as Urdu—but as Mr. Lyman talked, the fog parted a little. There was a clearing through which he could spy the plain outline of an intelligible system.

It is a good thing that the man can talk well,

for he has been selected as the narrator of the world match on Channel 13's exhaustive television coverage of the Bobby Fischer-Boris Spassky match, which will often require five continuous hours of talk—analyses, interviews, demonstrations and illuminating asides.

"Even a person who doesn't understand chess can watch it as a sporting event," Mr. Lyman said. "It's like watching a hockey game on television without knowing anything about hockey—just as a contest. Well, there's an ebb and flow to chess in terms of aggression, attack and defense. The white pieces go this way and the black pieces go that way—that's very easy to pick up.

"The game, as it takes place, has constant confrontations in terms of attack and defense. You have the equivalent of sudden death all the time late in the game.

"There was a radio match between the United States and England some years ago. The match hinged on one game. There are eight ranks on a chess board, and the issue became for the audience whether a pawn that was advancing toward the last rank could make it safely and become a queen.

"For a couple of hours, a whole radio audience was hanging on the edge of their seats, fascinated with this pawn that was slowly advancing, one move at a time, one square at a time, to the eighth rank. There was tremendous excitement and identification with the pawn.

"You can just look at a chess board and see pieces attacking or defending, pieces counterattacking. You see the struggle in terms of patterns of white and black pieces on the board.

"Chess is two armies marshaling their forces on a disputed terrain."

By now it was plain that Mr. Lyman was not going to use any petty rote-and-rules method of introducing the tyro to chess. The approach was more Churchillian, having to do with concepts and strategies.

At the practical level, it was like the speak-no-English method of learning a foreign language: no grammar, no principles, no explanations—just start talking.

A chess novice, suddenly thrown into association with a chess master, explores the comforts of the relationship of the spider and the fly, from a fly's-eye view.

After 35 minutes of rapid, learned talk, Mr. Lyman said suddenly: "Let's set up a game. This is really a gamble."

If it's a gamble for you, the tyro thought, what is it going to be for me?

Mr. Lyman's hands disappeared under the table, then came back up. The novice was offered a choice of two closed fists. He touched the right fist and received a black chess piece.

"You're Black, I'm White," Mr. Lyman said. "White always goes first. That gives White the initiative, and a good player can sometimes maintain that initiative all the way through against a weak opponent.

"I'm going to show you a movement on the board without explaining it in detail. See if you can follow. I'm not going to explain the rules."

"I'm going to play you, but you're not going to tell me the rules—wonderful," the novice said.

"Watch," Mr. Lyman said pleasantly. "I'm going to show you a game just as if I was teaching on television and you were at home watching. So you can't talk."

"Ah, a rule," the novice said. "I can't talk."

"This is really an epic battle," the teacher said, moving the pawns and pieces—knights, bishops, rooks, the queen and the king—rapidly through a game that he took from a book.

"Each piece has different powers: It can make different movements on the 8-by-8 board," Mr. Lyman said. "The chess board represents a a terrain and space, and the pieces move over that terrain on verticals, horizontals and diagonals.

"You see the rook here: It moves on verticals and horizontals. It can move in a straight line as far as it can go on the board.

"A good mnemonic device is that the rook is too thick a piece to get through the narrow points connecting the squares on the diagonal, so it can't move that way.

"But look at the bishop. It has a narrow waist, so it moves on the diagonals only."

As Mr. Lyman went on, making and explaining moves, it came out that:

The queen can move in any direction—vertical, horizontal or diagonal—any number of available spaces, making it the most powerful piece on the board.

The pawn is the only individual that can't move backward. It moves one square forward at a time (except on the first move, when it can go one or two squares) but is allowed to veer off on the diagonal to capture an enemy piece.

The knight has an eccentric gait. It can go left or right, moving in an L-shaped pattern—that is, it can go two squares up and one over, or one square over and two up, and it can jump over a piece in the process.

The king can go one space in any direction—vertical, horizontal or diagonal. It therefore holds power over an eight-square field—the two squares to either side of it, three squares in the row above, and three squares in the row below.

A player can capture an enemy piece if it is on a square that he can move to. All of the pieces, therefore, have varying fields of power on the board.

If each of these fields were seen separately and then superimposed on all the others, the complexity of chess could be seen for a single move.

"Every piece captures the way it moves—if it can go to a square, it can capture what is on that square," Mr. Lyman remarked. The pawn, the novice recalled in an unexpected flash of abstractive reasoning, is the exception, capturing on a bias though permitted to move only straight ahead.

"You may analyze 10 or 20 moves ahead," Mr. Lyman said. "That's rare, but it does happen. The possibilities branch out. Say you're analyzing six moves ahead. Each of those moves has six possibilities at least, so by the time you get to the sixth move you have six to a very high power."

Mr. Lyman went from the apparently infinite—the chess moves—to the obviously finite—the chess player.

"There's the pressure of time in chess," he said. "Your opponent is a person with a finite mind, a finite intelligence and character weaknesses, who has to try to cover a situation that cannot be completely covered in the time allotted.

"It's a struggle—chess is a battle and a struggle of wills. In the pressure of a game a player's heartbeat, respiration, blood pressure will change.

"One of the variables is your opponent's psychology. So you attack a person's psychological weaknesses. You put him under tremendous strain, push him to where he consumes his energy, where he gets exhausted.

"When he reaches a point of demoralization, a player can crash, go to pieces, lose.

"Bobby Fischer says he waits for the moment when his opponent's ego is crushed."

Mr. Lyman moved the pieces on the board, creating essentially a blur of impressions for the novice. Now and then a sentence could be snatched out of the stream-of-consciousness narration:

"In setting up the board, the white queen goes on the white space and the black queen on the black space," he said. The novice liked that. It was simple, clear, mnemonically perfect.

"You fight for the center of the board because a piece in the center controls more squares," he said.

"When the king is attacked and can't escape, you have checkmate and the game is completed."

Mr. Lyman showed a move, then demonstrated alternatives to the move. "That wouldn't work," he said.

"Why?"

"You can't talk," he shot back.

"It's like learning the piano and the violin—you never stop," Mr. Lyman remarked. "But you can learn the rules in half an hour."

"Not if you don't tell me, I can't," the novice murmured.

"As a teacher, I specialize in teaching people who are beginners," the master said in one reassuring breath. But a breath later, he noted that in chess a beginner is somebody "who already knows the moves."

"We're ready to play," he said, setting up the board again.

He moved. The novice moved. He moved. The novice moved.

"By the way," Mr. Lyman said, "the move you just made is exactly the one Fischer made in two games."

What a class the novice was in! Fischer himself could not have done better on the move! It must have gone to his head. His next move was not so good.

"I have four pieces on that square," Mr. Lyman said coolly, "This one, this one, this one and that one."

The novice quickly pulled back. He muttered that he could see only a few of the manifold possibilities on the board, and he could not see at all what the consequences of any move he made would be.

Mr. Lyman made his moves and he made the novice's, which turned out to be a disastrous collaboration for the black side.

There was an inexorable march of white pieces past the center and into black territory. On and on the white tide came, while a terrible inertia had seized the black pieces.

"When you see the pieces mass, even though

you don't know the rules, you can see I'm attacking," Mr. Lyman said.

Yes, the novice could see that.

"Suffered your first loss," Mr. Lyman said a little later, extending his hand across the board. He had won in 11 moves. He could have won in six, he said, if he had taken full advantage of the novice's ignorance and played unsoundly aggressive chess.

"From the moment you start to play, the smallest error can be fatal in a top-level game," Mr. Lyman said. "When the first pieces begin to move out on either side, a precarious situation is immediately created. You can't relax your attention for a moment.

"The essential quality of a high-level player is a kind of enjoyment of a very intense, physically and mentally exhausting struggle. Chess players aren't necessarily mathematical, or artistic, or more intelligent. Rather than any particular quality or mental ability, it's the ability to use every quality you have, every attribute and every character trait in the struggle against another person.

"Chess is rather unique in the way it lets people experience themselves in a whole way, as man the doer, man the maker. It's really like making love. You experience yourself, and you feel whole afterward."

"One thing I can tell you," the novice told his boss that night. "Checkers it isn't."

No serious attempt was made to teach the reader the fundamentals of chess. Periodical editors assumed—probably correctly—that such basics were really best left to books, or to friends willing to spend an evening with the would-be chess player. And teaching the rock-bottom fundamentals—how the pieces move and capture—would have been a futile gesture anyhow, because "knowing the moves" is to playing chess what knowing the twenty-six letters of the alphabet is to writing sonnets. Still, newspapers could, aside from reporting news of the chess battle itself, perform some useful functions. Such as presenting a glossary of commonly found words—words likely to crop up in coverage of a chess battle.

A glossary appeared in *The Times* of July 24th. Here it is, in somewhat expanded form:

> Because chess has been played so long, a tangle of terminology has grown up around it.
>
> Like newcomers to Russian novels who abandon plot and prose because they can't cope with the cast of trinomial characters (Rodion Rodionovich Raskolnikov, Afanasy Ivanovitch Vahrushin, *et al.*), would-be chess students have been known to turn back in the face of the verbal undergrowth (King's Fianchetto, Maroczy Bind, etc.).
>
> It is, of course, quite possible to play chess by ear, so to speak, without bothering with the niceties of names.
>
> But playing chess is one thing and reading about it is quite another, and when it comes to reading there is, alas, no way to avoid at least some of the technical terminology.
>
> Most of the words that crop up are people words. Like Ruy Lopez, for example.
>
> This is an opening system named after a 16th-century Spanish cleric and chess player, Ruy Lopez de Seguri, who—so the story goes—advised his chess students to, among other things, play only after their opponents had eaten and drunk heavily.
>
> The Lopez is characterized by the following moves:
>
> 1 P-K4   P-K4
> 2 N-KB3   N-QB3
> 3 B-N5
>
> And this is an example of terminology that cannot be avoided—symbolic notation.
>
> The notation is less formidable than it looks. The letters stand for the chessmen: K for king, Q for queen, B for bishop, N for knight, R for rook and P for pawn.

The numbers at the left are the moves of the game, the left-hand columns representing White's moves and the right-hand column Black's.

The hyphen means "moves to." Thus 1 P-K4 translates as "On his first turn, White moves his pawn to the fourth square on the king file." The N-QB3 means "On his second turn, Black moves a knight to the third square in his queen-bishop file."

Some symbols do not appear in the brief description of the Lopez opening. For example, the symbol "x," which means "captures." Thus, the notation BxN means "bishop captures knight." Often, a piece is in a position to capture more than one enemy man that can be symbolized with the same letter: A knight, for example, might be in a position to capture any of several enemy pawns. If it does capture one, how does the reader know which one was captured?

No sooner asked than done. If one of the capturable pawns is on the third rank (see "rank" in the glossary that follows) and one on the fourth, and the knight decides to pick off the one on the fourth, the move is notated as NxP/4, or "the knight captures the pawn on the fourth rank." Or take the example of a pawn that has an option of capturing, say, the enemy's bishop pawn or the enemy's queen pawn. To make the move clear, the chess notator would write—if such was indeed what happened—PxQP, meaning "pawn captures queen pawn."

And one more example of how ambiguities are resolved in symbolic form. A bishop may be in a position to capture a rook on either of two files (see "file" in the glossary)—the rook or bishop file, for instance. If it captures the rook on the bishop file, the move is written as BxR/B.

A move that attacks the king—called a "check"—is notated with the abbreviation "ch" following the move, as in R-Q6ch. If a piece is moved and, in being moved, unmasks an attack on the king by a different piece, the abbreviation "dis ch," meaning "discovered check," follows the move. And—oh formidable blow!—if a piece is moved and, in being moved, not only gives check, but also uncovers a check by another piece, the symbol "dbl ch," for "double check," is used.

When three dots appear before a move (as in "if 16 . . . N-B3") the move is one made by Black, the dots taking the place of the White move.

This leaves only O-O, which means "castles (see the glossary again) on the king's side," and O-O-O, which means "castles on the queen's side."

That, basically, is all there is to notation. Sometimes, however, some arabesques are added, such as Q-Q8! The "!" means the move is powerful, or winning. Or at least it is in the mind of the chess writer.

If it is not clear whether the move is a stroke of genius or a blunder—what is called a "strong but risky" move in chess language—the writer puts "!?" after the move as in N-N4!?

Permutations and combinations of !'s and ?'s can be used to indicate surprise, approbation, awe, puzzlement or—obviously—permutations and combinations of those feelings.

With the worst—the notation—out of the way, the rest is easy. Here then, is a sampling of terms that turn up from time to time.

BOOK

The written body of high-level chess play. "Book" moves are standard. A book player memorizes openings and their variations, and goes to pieces if his opponent strays from the accepted line.

CASTLE

A combined move of king and rook permitted once for each side during a game. The king moves two squares to either side, and the rook toward which it moves is placed on the square the king passed over. This is the only move in which the king moves more than one square at a time and in which more than one piece is moved. Castling cannot be done when the king has already moved, when the affected rook has already moved, when the king is in check, when the square over which the king must pass is under attack,

Initial position before castling.

Position after castling on the king's side (0-0).

Position after castling on the queen's side (0-0-0).

when the king would be in check after the move was completed, or when any of the squares between the king and the affected rook are occupied.

CENTER

The four squares in the geometrical center of the board. The opening moves are meant to gain control of the center.

CLOCK

Paired clocks used in all sanctioned tournaments and in many club games. After a player moves he punches a lever that stops his clock and starts his opponent's. Each clock, therefore, registers only the elapsed time for one player. If a player exceeds the time limit set on his clock, a flag falls and he loses the game, even if he has a winning position.

CLOSED GAME

One in which the maneuvering is tight and the pieces, as a rule, lack long-range operating space. Such games are sometimes called "positional," because they are quiet, with the opponents struggling for subtle advantages, rather than open and alive with tactical possibilities.

COMBINATION

A series of moves which, unless the player has miscalculated, will force an immediate win or an overwhelming advantage. A combination sometimes starts with a sacrifice of material.

DEVELOPMENT

The process of moving pieces from their starting positions so they can protect their own territory and put pressure on the opponent.

DIAGONAL

A row of squares running obliquely across the board rather than up and down (a file) or side to side (a rank).

DISCOVERED ATTACK

A player, by moving a piece, uncovers an attack on an opponent's piece. If the attacked piece is the king, the move is called discovered check.

DOUBLED PAWNS

Two pawns in tandem on the same file. Ordinarily a liability because, unable to protect each other, they are vulnerable.

DOUBLED ROOKS

Two rooks in tandem on the same file. Because they protect each other and act in concert, their power is more than double the power of a single rook.

END-GAME

The final stages of a game. Most pieces have

disappeared from the board, and the king, instead of hiding, becomes an active participant.

EN PASSANT

From the French, "in passing." Abbreviated e.p. One pawn can capture another e.p. if the capturing pawn has reached the fifth rank and the captured pawn is moved two squares forward on an adjacent file. The capture is made as though the opponent's pawn had moved only one square forward.

EN PRISE

French again. A piece is en prise when it is left exposed to capture with nothing to show for it.

EXCHANGE

The trading of a minor piece (bishop or knight) for a rook. To sacrifice the exchange is to trade the rook for the minor piece.

FIANCHETTO

A bishop played to the side of the board is said to be fianchettoed. Usually, the bishop is played to N2, from which position it sweeps along the long diagonal to the opponent's R1 square. The word is from the Italian fianco—the flank or side.

FILE

The rows running from player to player, named for the pieces that occupy them at the start of the game. From left to right they are, for White, the queen rook file, queen knight file, queen bishop file, queen file, king file, king bishop file, king knight file, king rook file. The order, read from right to left, is correct for the black side.

FORK

An attack on two or more pieces simultaneously. Though any chess piece—except a rook pawn—can execute a fork, the knight makes a specialty of it.

GAMBIT

An opening maneuver in which a pawn is offered in return for a strong position or a chance to attack.

GOOD BISHOP

A bishop free to operate without interference from its own pawns.

INDIAN DEFENSES

A family of openings in which Black replies 1 . . . N-KB3 to White's 1 P-Q4. There does not seem to be much agreement on the origin of the term, but most historians believe it derives from the style of play in India where—because pawns did not have the right to make a two-square initial move—games tended to be leisurely and conservative.

INTERPOSE

To place a pawn or piece between an attacked king and the attacking piece.

KING'S PAWN OPENING

The move 1 P-K4. Bobby Fischer's favorite opening. Moving the king pawn opens lines for the king bishop and the queen, occupies a key central square and prevents the opponent from occupying squares diagonally in front of the pawn.

MAJOR PIECES

The queen and rooks. Because of the number of squares they command (a queen can command 27 squares, not counting the one she occupies, a rook 14) they are considered the heavy artillery of chess.

MASTER, GRANDMASTER

The highest rankings in chess, earned by competing in major tournaments. There are about 90 grandmasters in the entire world.

MATING NET

A position or series of moves that leads inexorably to one in which the king must be mated.

MATE OR CHECKMATE

A position in which a king is attacked and cannot escape. The end of the game.

MIDDLE GAME

The phase of the game following the development, and the one in which much of the action takes place. With many pieces on the board and possibilities of attack on all sides, the king normally stays well hidden in this phase.

MINOR PIECES

The bishops and knights. A knight can command 8 squares, a bishop 13.

MOBILITY

The ability to move about freely on the board.

NIMZO-INDIAN DEFENSE

One of the Indian defenses, characterized by the sequence: 1 P-Q4, N-KB3; 2 P-QB4, P-K3; 3 N-QB3, B-N5. Named after Aron Nimzovitch, author of a book modestly titled *My System*. One of the many stories about Nimzovitch is that, in a losing position, during a tournament, he swept the pieces off the board and thundered, "Why must I lose to this idiot?"

OPEN FILE

A file cleared of pawns. It offers a corridor for attack, especially if occupied by doubled rooks.

OPENINGS

The more-or-less standardized and analyzed patterns of moves that both sides make at the start of a game. Some are named after people (Ruy Lopez), some after places (Budapest Counter-Gambit), some after pieces or moves (Four Knights

Defense). Some are descriptive (Giuoco Piano, or quiet game).

OPPOSITION

A position in which opposing kings stand on the same rank, file or diagonal, separated from each other by only one square. The player whose move brings the kings into opposition holds an advantage that, in an end-game, can be decisive.

PASSED PAWN

A pawn unopposed, on its own or adjacent files, by a pawn of another color. By being advanced to the eighth rank it can become any piece its owner chooses. A passed pawn, therefore, is a source of worry for the other side and a precious advantage for its owner. Two united passed pawns on adjacent files constitute a formidable weapon.

PERPETUAL CHECK

A sort of infinite cycle in which one side gives check, the other side gets out of check, the first side checks again in the same way—being unable to do otherwise without risking the loss of the game—and so on. It constitutes a draw.

PIN

A position in which a piece may not be moved because another piece would be subject to capture. If the piece subject to capture is the king, the pin is absolute and the pinned piece cannot legally be moved.

POSITIONAL CHESS

See *closed game*.

QUEENING

The promoting of a pawn that has reached the eighth rank. Ordinarily, a pawn is made a queen, since this is the most powerful piece. But sometimes a pawn is promoted to a lesser rank, especially if promotion to a queen would bring about a stalemate.

RANK

A row of squares running from side to side of the board Each side numbers the ranks from one to eight, starting with thc rank nearest him and running to the rank nearest his opponent.

ROOK

The piece that looks like and is sometimes called a castle. This can be confusing, because "castle," in chess, is a verb.

SICILIAN DEFENSE

Probably the most frequently played Black defense to 1 P-K4. Its characteristic move is 1 . . . P-QB4. The theory behind the tactic is that it is an aggressive attacking move, involving, ultimately, the opening of the queen-bishop file for Black. The Maroczy Bind (named after Geza Maroczy, a Hungarian master) is a variation of the Sicilian.

STALEMATE

A situation in which one side is unable to make a legal move although the king is not in check. A stalemate is a draw.

STAUNTON

A pattern of chessmen—the ordinary design found in plastic, wood, jade or whatever—named after Howard Staunton (1810–1874), a British chess champion who was challenged by Paul Morphy, the New Orleans-born chess genius. Staunton was more or less the unofficial world champion, but if his willingness to meet Morphy over the board is any indication, he kept his title more by footwork than by chessboard skill.

STRATEGY

The "master plan" of a game, as opposed to the tactics—the carrying out of that plan.

TEMPO

As in music, time. Plural, tempi. In chess, there are basically three elements—space, time and material. Space and material are self-evident. Time, however, is more subtle. Initially, White, having the first move, has a time advantage (and thus, the initiative). But White can, by making useless moves, waste time. To make a wasteful move is to "lose a tempo." Over the board, tempi, space and material can be exchanged back and forth for one another.

VARIATIONS

Departures from the accepted or standardized lines. But variations—if they have any value—often end up standardized themselves.

WON GAME

A position in which one side, if it does not blunder, ought to go on to checkmate the other. Winning a won game is sometimes impossible for beginners, but ought to be a foregone conclusion for grandmasters—which is why grandmasters often resign in positions that do not look hopeless to beginners.

ZUGZWANG

A situation in which a player would prefer not to move at all. Since the rules require a move on his turn, the player is forced to weaken his position.

Bit by bit, story by story, article by article, the world was kept informed, and a detailed picture of the complex, competitive, combative, compulsive (and sometimes convulsive) universe of chess was drawn. Those who had followed it all along knew much of the detail, but even they were unprepared for the events that unfolded after that spring day in Russia in 1969.

PART ONE/Background

1 How the Masters Compete

On June 17, 1969, a brilliant young Soviet chess star named Boris Spassky defeated Tigran Petrosian, one of his compatriots, before a respectfully enthralled audience in Moscow and thereby became the chess champion of the world. But even as the curtain was going down on the last act of the drama on the stage of Moscow's Estrada Theater, it was going up elsewhere in the world in simultaneous, or nearly simultaneous, prologues to a new drama that would, before it ended, seize the world's attention as it had never before been seized by the ancient and honorable, but often benignly neglected, game of chess.

Under the laws of the Fédération Internationale des Echecs—FIDE, the International Chess Federation—the world champion must defend his title every three years, and the process of selecting a challenger, like chess itself, is complex and time-consuming. It begins at about the time the new champion is being crowned, and every step is carefully regulated by FIDE.

But it wasn't always that way.

Though chess itself goes back at least a thousand years and possibly more (there is more speculation than scholarship in anything that pretends to be much more precise), there have been world champions in a formal sense only since 1886, when the Bohemian Wilhelm Steinitz defeated Johannes Zuckertort of Poland in a match in London. Until then there had been any number of outstanding players—Allgaier, Philidor, Deschapelles, Staunton, Anderssen, Morphy—but competition was offhand and even haphazard, with one player challenging another and some claiming championship status on little more than the basis of ego.

Steinitz and Zuckertort were generally conceded to be the world's strongest players at the time of their match, and thus its outcome—though it was not preceded by any organized eliminations—determined the world championship.

Steinitz successfully defended his title in several set matches, losing it, finally, to Emanuel Lasker in 1894. (There were, of course, then as earlier, many tournaments in which several players competed, round-robin style, but these had only a casual connection with world championship contests.) Lasker held the title for 27 years, through a long series of matches with powerful players (including the American Frank J. Marshall in 1907). When he lost it at last, in 1921, it was to the suave and dashing José Raoul Capablanca, who competed between assignments for the Cuban foreign service. Capablanca, in turn, was defeated in 1927 by Alexander Alekhine, a Russian expatriate (he became a French citizen in 1929), lawyer, eccentric and egomaniac. Alekhine lost the title in 1935 to Max Euwe of the Netherlands—now the president of FIDE—but recaptured it two years later in a return match.

Then, on March 24, 1946, just before the start of a scheduled world championship match with Mikhail Botvinnik of the Soviet Union, Alekhine died in Lisbon, throwing the status of the world chess championship into confusion, if not chaos. Did Botvinnik automatically take over the title? Did he have to play Euwe? Was Euwe entitled to claim the championship?

The death of Alekhine brought into bold relief the shortcomings of organized—or disorganized—chess. There was no accepted method for dealing with the situation, no set of rules and regulations setting out the process of succession, with or without the deaths of champions. Thus, Alekhine's death forced the chess world's hand.

FIDE, which was conceived at a congress in Zurich in 1922 and born in Paris two years later, acted with commendable speed and firmness, despite its still shaky international standing.

After Alekhine's death, it organized a four-round tournament to be held the following year in the Netherlands and—more importantly—it drew up a detailed plan for a three-year cycle of world championship elimination contests, with the first cycle to begin at about the same time the new champion was to be crowned.

Almost everything that could have gone wrong did

go wrong. FIDE was accused of drawing up an unworkably complicated plan, of making its proposals without proper representation from interested nations (the Soviet Union was not, at that time, a FIDE affiliate, and the United States was not represented at the decision-making congress) and of being generally highhanded about the whole thing.

Still, the world chess throne was vacant and something had to be done about it. In 1947 another congress was held (this time with the participation of the United States and of the Soviet Union, which had affiliated its chess federation with FIDE) and the original plans, with some modifications, were resurrected.

The four-lap tournament was held in March and April, 1948, split between the Hague and Moscow, and Botvinnik emerged as the new world champion. The runners-up were Vasily Smyslov and Paul Keres of the Soviet Union, Samuel Reshevsky of the United States and Dr. Euwe.

The three-year plan was already under way, and—though there have been many changes—it still forms the basic framework for the selection of a world champion. Then, as now, it consists basically of a series of preliminary tournaments and matches designed to cull the world's most able players and to bring one to the top of the heap. From time to time details are refined, changes are made, unforeseen contingencies crop up, and rules to cope with them are incorporated into the FIDE laws. But the essence of the system remains what it was when it was drawn up by that first, sorely pressed group in 1946. It works this way:

Before the end of calendar year in which the championship match takes place, regional tournaments are held in each of the ten regions into which FIDE divides the world. These are the zonal tournaments (the United States, Canada and the Soviet Union are separate zones; the remaining seven zones take in several countries each). Winners and, in some cases, runners-up, in the zonals then participate in an interzonal tournament. The top six winners of the interzonal then compete in a candidates' contest, together with the winner and runner-up of the previous candidates' contest (there are provisions for deaths, resignations, refusals to play, substitutions and other possibilities). The eight players are paired in a quarterfinal series of matches. Those who emerge victorious from the quarterfinals are paired again in a semifinal. The two players left from the semifinals then meet in a final match, the winner of which becomes the challenger of the world champion.

This system—of pairing the eight final challengers in individual knockout matches—was adopted in 1965. Before then, the candidates had played in a four-lap round-robin, with the top scorer becoming the challenger for the world title. Bobby Fischer, then as now the *enfant terrible* of the chess world, charged that the Russians were in collusion, agreeing to draw with each other while playing no-holds-barred games with non-Russians, and to do nothing to jeopardize the position of whichever one of them was leading. Fischer's charge, whether based on fact or fancy, could not be cavalierly dismissed, and the matter was taken up at the 1962 FIDE congress, which voted to change to the knockout match system as of 1965.

Thus the world championship of chess is now determined in a series of carefully regulated, supervised and documented steps. There are weaknesses in the system, as there are in almost anything dreamed up by man or woman, but FIDE tries to correct the defects.

About one thing there is no question: The present system is far superior to the one that permitted Howard Staunton to call himself the champion of the world although he refused to play Paul Morphy, the New Orleans-born genius who had swept through America and Europe decimating the finest players the world had to offer. Morphy should have been the champion (among those he defeated in match play was Adolph Anderssen, who shared with Staunton the unofficial world championship) but was not. He went back home never having met Staunton over the chessboard. There seems little doubt that, had the present system been used back in the 1800's, Morphy would have been what Bobby Fischer is today, the first American chess champion of the world.

2 Fischer Fever

The international chess rules are quite clear: The regional contests—the zonals—that are the first step in the three-year cycle for the world championship must begin before the end of the year in which the championship itself is decided. And for the zonals to finish before the end of the year, the organizing and maneuvering that precedes them must get under way before the fall.

And so it was in the summer of '69. The new champion of the world, Boris Spassky, a 32-year-old journalist from Leningrad, was enjoying his new status in a modest way. The long, punishing tournaments and matches were behind him and he would face no more challenges (or none, at least, that would have a bearing on his official position in the world of chess) for three years.

But in Zones 1 through 10, as drawn up by FIDE, the race was on. In the United States, officially designated Zone 5, the Zonal Tournament was one and the same with the United States Chess Championship Tournament. That event, played in a midtown Manhattan office building, drew the cream of the country's players.

There was Reshevsky, the Polish-born onetime child chess prodigy and six times the United States champion. There was Father William Lombardy, once the world junior champion, and Larry Evans, the peripatetic and articulate defending champion. And Pal Benko, who had fled Hungary and since then won the U. S. Open Chess Championship four times.

But the brightest star of them all, Bobby Fischer, who had won his first U. S. championship at the age of 14 and who had won it seven more times since then, was not there. Fischer—whose international match and tournament record had been headed for new heights, who had sworn that the only thing between him and the world championship was the conniving of the Russians—was out of it. He had walked out of the Interzonal Tournament at Sousse, Tunisia, on November 5, 1967, by failing to show up for the 15th round. He had been ahead of the 22 others at the time, with a score of 13½–1½, and all he would say through his locked hotel-room door when asked for an explanation was: "Leave me in peace. I have nothing to say."

That had been his last formal appearance, and he had, in a sense, become something close to a recluse. Though he had said before, several times, that he coveted the world title, his refusal to participate in the United States championship meant he had foreclosed his chances—for this cycle—of capturing that title.

The tournament began on November 30, 1969, and the first point in the 12-man round-robin was scored by Bernard Zuckerman, an international master from Brooklyn. He defeated a grandmaster, Arthur Bisguier of Hartsdale, N. Y.

The lead and runner-up spots shifted back and forth in the next 17 days and, when the tournament ended on December 17 to the applause of about 100 previously restrained and respectfully silent chess fans in the audience, Reshevsky was the winner with 7 points out of a possible 11, and a $2,000 prize. William G. Addison, an international master from San Francisco, was second and Benko third.

Reshevsky, Addison and Benko thus qualified for the coming Interzonal, the next step in the championship eliminations. All three were delighted. But there were chess players and chess followers around the world who—while not begrudging the three winners their laurels—felt that without Fischer the United States would not really be represented in the Interzonal. Among those dissatisfied people was Lt. Col. Edmund B. Edmondson, executive director of the United States Chess Federation and one of five elected members of the FIDE Bureau. Edmondson started working on what at the time looked like a hopeless—and quite possibly thankless—task: to convince Fischer to return to the active world of chess and then, having done that, to somehow get him into the Interzonal despite his having failed to qualify formally.

Edmondson, a soft-spoken, friendly man who had long been about as close to Fischer as almost anyone can get, did persuade him to return. Fischer agreed to play in a Russia vs. the World tournament and, to the amazement of Fischer-watchers, yielded first-board position to Bent Larsen, the Danish grandmaster. Playing in the No. 2 spot, Fischer rolled right over the Russian opposition, and this whetted his appetite—he was ready to play in the coming Interzonal, to get a chance to wrest the world title from the Russians. The problem became one of getting America's No. 1 chess star into the Interzonal.

Edmondson talked, discussed, bargained, made offers and heard counter-offers. Out of the maneuvering, horse trading and politicking emerged a resolution presented to and approved by the FIDE General Assembly. If one of the three Americans who had officially qualified would step down, said FIDE, Fischer would be allowed to take his place in the Interzonal.

"The moment Benko heard this," Edmondson said, "he volunteered to step aside."

But this did not mean that Fischer automatically was in. Edmondson was bound by the rules to ask all those who had finished in the first eight places in the U. S. championship if they were willing to cede their rights to Fischer.

Lombardy, who had placed fourth and who, ordinarily, would have moved up to a qualifying position if one of those ahead of him dropped out, was willing. Edmondson said that, when asked if he would give up his rights, the young Roman Catholic priest replied:

"You know I want to play in the Interzonal. I would step aside for only one person—and that's Fischer."

Lombardy did step aside, as did those who had finished in the fifth, sixth, seventh and eighth places. Fischer was seeded into the Interzonal and once more he was on his way toward the title he coveted—the title that had been safely in Soviet hands since 1948.

The Interzonal, with 24 competitors, got under way in Palma de Mallorca, Spain, on November 9, 1970. Those who finished in the first six places were to go on to the next step—the candidates' contests—together with Tigran Petrosian, the man Spassky had defeated for the world championship, and Viktor Korchnoi, the Soviet grandmaster who had been runner-up in the previous candidates' competition.

Fischer swept through the Interzonal, crushing his opponents in his last seven games and finishing with a score of 17½–5½, two and a half points ahead of his nearest rivals, Yefim Geller of the Soviet Union, Larsen and Robert Huebner of West Germany, who wound up in a three-way tie for second with 15–8 each.

Wolfgang Uhlmann of West Germany and Mark Taimanov of the Soviet Union rounded out the list of qualifiers.

Thus the stage was set for the last step before the championship match itself—the candidates' knockout matches. These were set to start on May 13, with these pairings:

Fischer and Taimanov would meet in Vancouver, British Columbia, Petrosian and Huebner in Seville, Spain, Larsen and Uhlmann in the Canary Islands, and Geller and Korchnoi in the Russian Black Sea resort city of Sochi. Each match in this quarterfinal series would consist of 10 games, with the first player to score 5½ or better the winner.

Dim hints of things to come were heard in Vancouver even before the Fischer-Taimanov match got under way there. Fischer demanded that spectators be barred, and Soviet officials protested that this violated international chess rules and that Taimanov would not play under those conditions. Dr. Euwe, the FIDE president, countered with a threat to drop Taimanov and substitute Lajos Portisch of Hungary, who had just missed qualifying in the Interzonal. The Soviet officials warned, in turn, that if Euwe made the substitution all the Soviet players in the candidates' matches—Geller, Petrosian and Korchnoi—would drop out.

Euwe stood his ground. Let them drop out, he said; he would replace the whole lot.

The Soviet delegation gave in, Fischer got his way and the match got under way—but not before both Fischer and Taimanov had the site changed. Taimanov had looked at the playing room and gasped, "I cannot breathe in this room." Fischer, too, was unhappy with it. The match sponsors found another site and the games at long last began.

Fischer had the black pieces in the first game. But unlike other players, from woodpushers to grandmasters, who try for no more than a draw when playing Black, Fischer went for the win. And he won.

In the second game, playing White, he won again. And then again in the third game.

Taimanov, by this time on the nil side of a 3–0 score, became ill. He called for a postponement to recover his health—and undoubtedly his composure. The postponement was granted and Taimanov took a few days off. It did not help. When the match resumed, the Soviet grandmaster lost the fourth, fifth and sixth games.

The match was over. Taimanov had been shut out, routed. Fischer had accomplished the unheard-of: He had won a match with a grandmaster without suffering one loss or allowing one draw.

And Taimanov, though he did not know it at the time, had become the first victim of a strange and controversial malady that did not yet have a name but that was soon to have several.

The victory over Taimanov gave Fischer a record of 13 consecutive victories in grandmaster play—the seven final games at Palma and the six straight against Taimanov.

The other survivors of the quarterfinals were Petrosian (Huebner had withdrawn part-way through because of ill health), Larsen and Korchnoi. In the next round, the semifinals, Larsen would meet Fischer and Petrosian would meet Korchnoi.

The Petrosian-Korchnoi match, played in Moscow, went the way grandmaster matches often went and were expected to go. The first game was a draw, as was the second. Then the third, fourth, fifth, sixth, seventh and eighth games were drawn. Nobody was taking any chances. Petrosian was playing his usual cautious game; Korchnoi was willing to keep things on an even keel. At the end of eight games, the score was even at 4–4.

Then, in the ninth game, Petrosian won, putting

him ahead by one point, 5–4. And the two games that followed were drawn, making the final score Petrosian 5½, Korchnoi 4½.

But in Denver, where Fischer and Larsen—who was generally considered second in strength only to Fischer among Western players—were confronting each other, the pattern was different.

In the first game, on July 6, Fischer, playing White, began with the move he had used in almost every tournament and match game he had ever played—P-K4. Larsen, a cool and confident Danish engineer, replied with 1 . . . P-K3, the French Defense, an opening that no one watching the match could remember having seen Larsen use in years.

If the reply was meant to surprise Fischer and knock him off balance, it didn't work. The American grandmaster made his next moves rapidly, gained control of the center and castled his king into safety.

Larsen, trying for counterplay in the center, threatened one of Fischer's pawns; Fischer made no effort to protect it, choosing to continue his development, and Larsen took the pawn. He soon regretted it, for he found his king unable to castle and in a precarious position.

Fischer, however, missed the best line and Larsen's game took on new life. With his queen and a rook on aggressive lines, Larsen gave up two minor pieces for one of Fischer's rooks and subjected Fischer's king to a violent assault.

But Fischer, known for his prowess as an aggressive player, found the right defensive moves each time and came through with his game intact. At that point Larsen had four pawns to Fischer's two and a queen to Fischer's rook and two bishops.

What Fischer had that Larsen didn't have was a passed pawn. And Larsen was unable to stop it. He resigned on the 41st move.

The score was 1–0.

The second game, on July 8, went 54 moves, with Larsen attacking, defending and going into the endgame with a slight edge. But he slipped, making a move that was short of the best on his 35th turn. Fischer pounced on that minuscule error and forced an exchange that put him two pawns ahead of Larsen, who resigned.

The score was 2–0.

In the third game, Larsen slipped quickly—he made poor moves on his 11th and 12th turns—but he played on, trying to recoup. After 41 moves he resigned.

The score: 3–0.

The fourth game lasted 33 moves, though it ended, in effect, on the 24th move, when Larsen retreated a knight and gave Fischer a target to zero in on. At the end, Larsen's pawn chain lay in shambles and his queen, rook and king were being threatened simultaneously by a knight.

The score now: 4–0.

On July 13, with his chances of winning the match virtually nil—he would have had to win four games just to pull up even with Fischer—Larsen asked for a postponement on medical grounds. Like Taimanov, he had become ill.

The chess world was beginning to wonder. What was this illness that seemed to strike Fischer's opponents? Why did they sag and then collapse? Why did they play so poorly? Why did they grow physically ill? What was this Fischer mystique—this affliction that the American grandmaster Robert Byrne later was to call "Fischer Fear" and that others would call "Fischer Fever"?

Other strong players had noticed that kind of phenomenon before, though never on the epidemic scale it now seemed to be assuming. Grandmasters in the past had often remarked that they never managed to defeat anyone who was in good health. The player on the losing end always, it seemed, was indisposed in some way and, of course, was not playing up to his usual good-health standards.

And so it was with Fischer and his opponents. The theme would run through Fischer's match and tournament record like a Wagnerian leitmotif: His opponents are not playing the way they normally do.

Or was it simply that Fischer was so good he made his opponents look bad?

The match resumed on July 18, and the fifth game went the way the previous four had gone. Larsen, unable to stop the advance of one of Fischer's pawns, gave up on the 46th move.

The score was now 5–0.

On July 20 Fischer and Larsen met for the sixth game on the stage of the 500-seat auditorium in Temple Buell College. The match sponsors had spent $1,500 just to provide special lighting fixtures for the players. Spectators were permitted only in the last few rows of the auditorium—to help maintain the silence and keep distractions to an absolute minimum—and 300 other fans watched on a demonstration board set up in an adjoining hall.

Larsen, though hopelessly behind with his 5-0 deficit, played hard. He used Bird's Opening, which was transposed into a form of the Sicilian. Fischer adopted, unexpectedly (he plays for the full point even when he needs only a draw), a defensive game. Larsen took command of the center and applied pressure on Fischer's position. On the 19th move, he sacrificed a pawn to keep his attack moving. His queen and bishop advanced on Fischer's king, and he moved his king rook forward.

Fischer, playing calmly, kept finding the correct defense. When Larsen offered a second pawn, Fischer accepted it. The move backfired on Larsen, and his attack faltered, then died. Fischer followed up with an exchange of pieces that, in the end-game, gave him the advantage of the two pawns that Larsen had sacrificed.

Larsen took a long look at the position, and resigned.

The score was 6–0. For the second time in a row Fischer had done what no one had ever done even once before—he had defeated a grandmaster in six straight games.

Fischer's winning streak now totaled 19 games. Only one hurdle remained between him and a chance to meet Spassky for the world title: Tigran Petrosian.

Petrosian, a genial, 42-year-old Armenian, had once been a street cleaner. He had also been the world chess champion for six years, having taken the title from Botvinnik in 1963 and having successfully defended it in '66 against Spassky.

Though he had been accused of playing lackluster chess, of being overly cautious, of being always the calculating defender instead of the daring attacker, his record was impressive. He had won the Soviet junior championship at 17 and, at 23, had become a grandmaster. He was not to be lightly dismissed.

In a sense, he was the very antithesis of both Larsen and Fischer. And perhaps, chess observers speculated, this kind of player—this careful, deliberate, solid, defensive kind of player—would be the kind to bring Fischer to his knees.

The Fischer-Petrosian match was scheduled to be played in Buenos Aires, with the first game to start on September 30, 1971. There were to be 12 games in all, with victory going to the first one to score more than 6 points.

Petrosian arrived in Buenos Aires on September 22 and told newsmen he considered Fischer "an aggressive player with brilliant innovations." But, he said confidently, he expected to find "the formula" to defeat him. (Some, at least, of Petrosian's compatriots did not share his optimism. Botvinnik said he expected Fischer to win and Tass, the official Soviet press agency, gave Fischer a slight edge.)

Among the aficionados gathered in Buenos Aires, the feeling was that Petrosian would follow in Taimanov's and Larsen's footsteps.

Petrosian and Fischer had met 18 times over the chessboard and were even, with 12 draws and three victories each. The record was neutral.

In the first game, Petrosian had the black pieces and he played the Sicilian Defense, an opening not associated with him. The Sicilian is a fighting game, and Petrosian is not a fighting player. On his 11th turn, he played P-Q4 and Fischer then proceeded cautiously, using up more than half an hour on his next few moves. Despite having the black side, Petrosian managed to seize the initiative by giving up a pawn, and Fischer's king seemed to be in danger.

But Fischer played carefully—the roles in that first game seemed to be reversed, with Petrosian trying new and daring and aggressive moves, and Fischer cautiously searching for the correct defensive replies—and he succeeded in equalizing.

On his 29th move, Petrosian sought a draw by repetition, but Fischer disdained it and found a way to develop winning chances through a passed king rook pawn. Petrosian's attempt at counterplay proved inadequate and, when his 40th turn came, he resigned.

Attack and defense, risk and caution, were not the only aspects that seemed reversed in that game. Shortly after the game started the lights above the stage failed—they were out for 15 minutes—and it was Petrosian, not Fischer, who complained to the referee, Lothar Schmid.

The score was now 1–0, and Fischer's winning streak totaled 20 games.

That incredible winning streak was finally snapped on October 5, when, in the second game, Fischer resigned on his 32nd turn in a Gruenfeld Defense. The moves of that game were as follows:

White Petrosian	Black Fischer	White Petrosian	Black Fischer
1 P-Q4	N-KB3	17 O-O	Q-R4
2 P-QB4	P-KN3	18 Q-B2	P-B5
3 N-QB3	P-Q4	19 P-B4	PxP
4 B-B4	B-N2	20 P-B5	Q-Q7
5 P-K3	P-B4	21 Q-R4ch	K-B1
6 QPxP	Q-R4	22 QR-Q1	Q-K7
7 R-B1	N-K5	23 P-Q6	Q-R4
8 PxP	NxN	24 P-B4	P-K7
9 Q-Q2	QxRP	25 PxB	PxQR(Q)
10 PxN	Q-R4	26 RxQ	QxP
11 B-B4	N-Q2	27 R-KB1	P-B3
12 N-K2	N-K4	28 Q-N3	K-N2
13 B-R2	B-B4	29 Q-B7ch	K-R3
14 BxN	BxB	30 PxP	P-B4
15 N-Q4	QxP/4	31 RxP	Q-Q5ch
16 NxB	PxN	32 K-R1	Resigns

Fischer's attitude must have played a part in his defeat. After those 20 consecutive victories he no doubt believed that all his opponents would eventually blunder or make a less-than-best move and that he would be able to take advantage of the lapse. Had he been playing for a draw, in "normal" Black fashion, he might have had little trouble. But he took a risk and missed.

Instead of 12 . . . N-K4, he could have played 12 . . . NxP, reaching an excellent deployment. Then, eventually, he could have castled, developed his queen bishop and brought pressure to bear on the queen bishop file, with excellent prospects. He seemed to have neglected to take into account the possibility of 14 BxN and 16 NxB, which left him with vulnerable pawns. The rapid opening of lines then gave White access to a direct attack against the Black king and Fischer—for the first time since the early stages of the Interzonal—folded.

Had the spell been broken? Had the Fischer mystique been unmasked as only the figment of some overworked imaginations? Speculation was running wild, not only in Buenos Aires among the spectators, but wherever chess fans gathered to discuss the games and the Fischer record and prospects.

The cautious, "lackluster" Petrosian, master of defense and eschewer extraordinary of daring play, the unexciting Petrosian had done what a long string of brilliant, aggressive grandmasters had failed to do. He had beaten Fischer and proved that the American was just another chess player and not the invincible machine that so many of his admirers—as well as his critics—were making him out to be.

The third, fourth and fifth games seemed to enforce the feeling that Fischer's hypnotic powers had vanished (if indeed he had ever had them). Those games were draws, and one of them—the fourth—was something totally unexpected of Fischer: a grandmaster draw that went only 20 moves.

The score, at the end of five games, stood even at 2½–2½. Interest in the match, which had been intense to start with, was at a fever pitch. Customers were getting on line at the San Martin Theater at nine in the morning (the games started at 5 P.M.) for the tickets, which were being rationed at two to a customer. Some tickets were being resold minutes after they were bought at double the official price of 3 pesos (60 cents). At times, 3,500 people were in line waiting to get to the box office.

The sixth game was the first to reach the five-hour time control and be adjourned to the following day, at the end of 41 moves. At adjournment, Fischer had the advantage—he had a rook, a bishop and five pawns to Petrosian's rook, knight and four pawns. Petrosian, living up to his reputation, was playing solidly, defensively, and had set up a blockade in the center. He was effectively holding Fischer at bay.

When the game resumed, Fischer ceded two pawns and, on his 59th turn, succeeded in getting his rook behind Petrosian's pawns, threatening Petrosian's king and knight and to advance his queen pawn.

With his position and his chances rapidly deteriorating, Petrosian sacrificed his knight for two pawns, hoping to exchange Fischer's remaining pawns for a drawish end-game. But Fischer sidestepped that possibility and launched a direct assault—a mating attack. On his 67th turn, Petrosian resigned.

These are the moves of the sixth game:

White Petrosian	Black Fischer	White Petrosian	Black Fischer
1 N-KB3	P-QB4	24 P-QR4	PxP
2 P-QN3	P-Q4	25 PxP	P-B5
3 B-N2	P-B3	26 PxP	N/3xBP
4 P-B4	P-Q5	27 NxN	NxN
5 P-Q3	P-K4	28 Q-K2	NxB
6 P-K3	N-K2	29 QxN	KR-N1
7 B-K2	KN-B3	30 Q-R2	B-N5
8 QN-Q2	B-K2	31 QxQch	KxQ
9 O-O	O-O	32 R-B7ch	K-K3
10 P-K4	P-QR3	33 P-N4	B-B6
11 N-K1	P-QN4	34 R-R2	R-QB1
12 B-N4	BxB	35 RxR	RxR
13 QxB	Q-B1	36 P-R5	R-QR1
14 Q-K2	N-Q2	37 P-R6	R-R2
15 N-B2	R-N1	38 K-B1	P-N4
16 KR-B1	Q-K1	39 K-K2	K-Q3
17 B-R3	B-Q3	40 K-Q3	K-B4
18 N-K1	P-N3	41 N-N1	K-N4
19 PxP	PxP	42 N-K2	B-R4
20 B-N2	N-N3	43 R-N2ch	KxP
21 N/1-B3	R-R1	44 R-N1	R-QB2
22 P-QR3	Q-B2	45 R-N2	B-K8
23 Q-Q1	N-R4	46 P-B3	K-R4

White Petrosian	Black Fischer	White Petrosian	Black Fischer
47 R-B2	R-QN2	58 R-QN7	R-QR1
48 R-R2ch	K-N4	59 RxP	R-R8
49 R-N2ch	B-N5	60 NxPch	PxN
50 R-R2	R-QB2	61 KxP	R-Q8ch
51 R-R1	R-QB1	62 K-K3	B-B4ch
52 R-R7	B-R4	63 K-K2	R-KR8
53 R-Q7	B-N3	64 P-R4	K-B5
54 R-Q5ch	B-B4	65 P-R5	R-R7ch
55 N-B1	K-R5	66 K-K1	K-Q6
56 R-Q7	B-N5	Resigns	
57 N-K2	K-N6		

The score was now 3½–2½.

In the seventh game, Petrosian again tried the uncharacteristic (for him) Sicilian Defense. On his fourth move, he varied from the pattern he had used in the first game, playing 4 . . . P-QR3 instead of 4 . . . N-QB3. The alternative 4 . . . N-KB3 would have been more forceful. Against it, White can defend with 5 N-QB3 but he has no time to develop his king bishop and set up a new pattern of deployment.

Twice, early in the game, Petrosian tried to create complications through sacrifices. The first was with 12 . . . Q-Q2. Had Fischer then played 13 B-QN5, the moves 13 . . . PxB; 14 QxR, O-O might have followed and Fischer would have gained a rook for a bishop but with a serious loss of time for his queen, which would have been in danger of being trapped.

The second effort was 15 . . . O-O. Here the reply 16 N-N6 could have led to 16 . . . QR-N1; 17 BxP, N-N5, netting a pawn for Fischer but giving Petrosian ample counterplay.

Fischer turned down both offers in favor of going on with his development and increasing the pressure on Petrosian's weak spots. On his 24th move Fischer planted a rook on the seventh rank. Petrosian tried briefly for counterplay on the king's wing, but it led nowhere, and, on his 34th move, he resigned.

The moves of the seventh game were:

White Fischer	Black Petrosian	White Fischer	Black Petrosian
1 P-K4	P-QB4	3 P-Q4	PxP
2 N-KB3	P-K3	4 NxP	P-QR3

White Fischer	Black Petrosian	White Fischer	Black Petrosian
5 B-Q3	N-QB3	20 P-B3	KR-R2
6 NxN	NPxN	21 R-K5	B-Q2
7 O-O	P-Q4	22 NxBch	RxN
8 P-QB4	N-B3	23 R-QB1	R-Q3
9 BPxP	BPxP	24 R-B7	N-Q2
10 PxP	PxP	25 R-K2	P-N3
11 N-B3	B-K2	26 K-B2	P-KR4
12 Q-R4ch	Q-Q2	27 P-B4	P-R5
13 R-K1	QxQ	28 K-B3	P-B4
14 NxQ	B-K3	29 K-K3	P-Q5ch
15 B-K3	O-O	30 K-Q2	N-N3
16 B-QB5	KR-K1	31 KR-K7	N-Q4
17 BxB	RxB	32 R-B7ch	K-K1
18 P-N4	K-B1	33 R-QN7	NxBP
19 N-B5	B-B1	34 B-B4	Resigns

The score now stood at 4½–2½.

Shortly after the game ended Petrosian asked for a postponement. He was ill, he said. The Fischer fever virus, which many thought had been weakened by the vaccine of the second Petrosian-Fischer game and wiped out by the third, fourth and fifth games, had returned, as virulent as ever, and Petrosian was its latest victim.

The Soviet star took four days to recuperate, returning to the stage of the San Martin Theater on October 24 for the eighth game of the match. His recovery was apparently not complete, for he lasted only 40 moves, despite having the advantage of the white pieces.

The score was now 5½–2½.

One of Petrosian's aides, the Soviet grandmaster Yuri Averbach, admitted after that eighth game that it was all over. Petrosian's spirit, he said, had been broken by the previous defeat. The Fischer mystique was in full operation.

The *coup de grace* was administered on October 26. Fischer lounged in his special chrome-and-leather swivel chair, occasionally leaning forward. Petrosian, his feet tucked primly under his chair, showed the tension now and then by suddenly gripping his head in both hands. From time to time, during Fischer's turns, Petrosian would step behind a screen and sip coffee from a vacuum flask. His wife, a small, roundish woman who had brewed the coffee for him, watched from a seat in the fourth row—the first three being kept vacant at Fischer's request.

The game was a classic example of building up a small advantage into a winning one. The opening was a French Defense, 1 . . . P-K3, played by Petrosian in response to Fischer's expected opening, 1 P-K4.

This is hardly the kind of opening expected of a player in a desperate position. Thus, in a paradoxical situation, Petrosian injected a move that had fallen into disuse—3 . . . N-QB3. Fischer promptly pinned the knight with 6 B-QN5 and Petrosian countered by pinning White's king knight. Fischer, however, relieved the pin by attacking Petrosian's bishop with 7 P-KR3, and when Petrosian exchanged with 7 . . . BxN, Fischer gained what is sometimes called the minor exchange—a bishop for a knight.

With 9 . . . P-QR3 Petrosian provoked an exchange that left him with doubled pawns, isolated and weak, and Fischer swarmed all over the weakness. His 21 P-QB4 opened lines leading to the weak area.

From there on it was little more than a mop-up operation for Fischer. With 27 RxP and 31 RxQP and 32 RxP, Black's men, his chances, his game and whatever slim hopes he might have had for the championship disappeared. There was a brief flurry when he tried to make Fischer believe he was weaving a mating net, but the charade was short-lived.

At the end, Petrosian was left with a pawn and knight to Fischer's five pawns—two united pawns on the queen's side and three on the king's. He had no way to stop Fischer and, on his 46th turn, he resigned.

Here are the moves of that last Fischer-Petrosian game.

White Fischer	Black Petrosian	White Fischer	Black Petrosian
1 P-K4	P-K3	6 B-QN5	B-KN5
2 P-Q4	P-Q4	7 P-KR3	BxN
3 N-QB3	N-QB3	8 QxB	B-K2
4 N-B3	N-B3	9 B-N5	P-QR3
5 PxP	PxP	10 BxNch	PxB

White Fischer	Black Petrosian	White Fischer	Black Petrosian
11 O-O	O-O	29 K-N3	N-R4ch
12 KR-K1	P-R3	30 K-R4	P-N3
13 B-R4	Q-Q2	31 RxQP	R-K1
14 R-K2	P-QR4	32 RxP	R/K-K8
15 QR-K1	B-Q1	33 N-B3	N-B5
16 P-QN3	R-N1	34 K-N4	N-K3
17 N-R4	N-K5	35 R-K5	P-B4ch
18 BxB	QRxB	36 K-N3	P-B5ch
19 Q-B4	Q-Q3	37 K-R4	K-R2
20 QxQ	PxQ	38 N-K4	P-N4ch
21 P-QB4	N-B3	39 K-N4	N-N2
22 R-QB1	R-N1	40 NxPch	PxN
23 PxP	PxP	41 RxR	RxR
24 P-B3	N-R4	42 KxP	N-K3ch
25 R-B6	N-B5	43 K-B5	R-K7
26 R-Q2	KR-K1	44 RxR	NxPch
27 RxP	R-K8ch	45 K-K5	NxR
28 K-B2	R-KR8	46 P-QR4	Resigns

Two days later, Fischer made a short but gracious speech at the theater, calling Petrosian "a good sport and a good opponent," accepted a medal, signed a few autographs, and then slipped out by the same back entrance he had used all along to avoid the chess fans who tried to find him and who, when they did, dogged his steps.

In Moscow's Central Chess Club the kibitzers were going over the games.

"Four games in a row," one of them said, referring to the four final games between Petrosian and Fischer. "That's hard to take."

"But," he added hopefully, "we've still got Spassky."

And, indeed, Spassky was next—the final door through which the American phenomenon would have to pass before entering the throne room of chess.

3 A War of Nerves

The Fischer-Petrosian match should have been the last exciting event before the start of the championship playoff itself. In one sense it was—there were no further chess games, no matches, no tournaments, involving the principals. But in a wider sense the defeat of Petrosian was only the starting signal for off-the-board maneuvers that would propel chess from obscure corners of inside pages in a handful of newspapers to the front pages of dailies from coast to coast and throughout the world.

Like a chess game itself, the opening moves were more or less routine. Under FIDE rules, the national federation of the challenger (in this case the United States Chess Federation) had the right to organize the first 12 games of the championship match; the defender's national federation had the right to organize the second half. Both sides could, under FIDE rules, agree on mutually satisfactory arrangements.

The international federation invited bids for the right to play host to the coming match, which was expected to be a considerable tourist attraction. By January 1, 1971, the deadline for the receipt of bids, ten nations and five cities had made offers. They were:

Colombia	$ 40,000
France	$ 50,000 plus 5 percent of the gross from television, film, admissions, souvenirs and travel packages involving the match.
Greece	$ 52,000
Switzerland	$ 60,000
Zagreb, Yugoslavia	$ 70,000
Canada	$ 75,000
The Netherlands	$ 80,000

Brazil	$ 80,000
West Germany	$ 92,000
Bled, Yugoslavia	$100,000
Chicago	$100,000
Sarajevo, Yugoslavia	$120,000
Iceland	$125,000
Argentina	$150,000
Belgrade, Yugoslavia	$152,000

In addition, Sebastian Leone, the Borough President of Brooklyn, offered $75,000 and Walter Goldwater, president of the Marshall Chess Club in Manhattan, threw in an extra $25,000.

Though there is disagreement about the size of some previous chess purses, the bids far eclipsed even the $20,000 record prize said to have been put up for the Lasker-Capablanca match. (Some chess chroniclers say the previous record was the $12,000 put up for the Fischer-Petrosian match in Buenos Aires. Still others say the record was really $5,000 offered near the turn of the century, which, in terms of real value, would be far higher today.) Spassky, when he defeated Petrosian in 1969, received $1,400.

The bids, opened at FIDE headquarters in Amsterdam, reflected the growing interest in chess, or at least in what was already known as the Fischer mystique. For his part, Fischer said of the bids that they were "not bad—they'll have to do." He declined to comment on his preference for a match site, saying this would be the subject of delicate negotiations in the coming weeks. "Delicate," as it turned out, was plainly the wrong adjective.

Earlier, before the bids had been received, Fischer had expressed the hope that an American city would be the high bidder. "I'm used to the climate and the people," he said, "but I wouldn't want to play in Brooklyn. Some other city, but not Brooklyn." His second choice, he said, was Canada.

But it was unlikely that Spassky would agree to play on American soil, just as it was unlikely that Fischer would be willing to meet Spassky on Soviet territory.

Nevertheless, Fischer said, he would play Spassky

whatever the site because "I want the money and I want the title even more."

Eventually, Argentina was dropped from the bidding, leaving Belgrade and Iceland as the two top contenders. That was because Fischer said he preferred Belgrade; Spassky said he would rather play in Iceland, where the climate would be closer to what it was in his native Leningrad.

The contestants had until February 10 to agree. Colonel Edmondson, the head of the United States Chess Federation, flew to Amsterdam, where he conferred with FIDE officials, and then to Reykjavik, where he spoke with Icelandic Chess Federation officers.

No agreement was reached and, on February 14, four days after the deadline, Dr. Euwe, president of FIDE, ruled that the championship match would be played partly in Belgrade and partly in Reykjavik. The match, he said, would start no later than June 25 in Belgrade and would shift to Iceland after the first 12 games. The purse would come to $138,500, a figure midway between Belgrade's bid of $152,000 and Iceland's $125,000, with the winner to get five-eighths and the loser three-eighths.

Spassky had submitted alternative choices of The Netherlands, France and Germany; Fischer's other selections were Montreal, Buenos Aires and Sarajevo.

The conditions originally laid down provided for one veto by each side of Dr. Euwe's ruling. However, the Soviet officials did not submit a full list of 15 match sites, in order of preference, saying that all but their four nominations—Iceland, The Netherlands, France and Germany—were unacceptable. Dr. Euwe ruled this to be an exercise of the veto power and therefore, he said, the Russians were entitled to no further vetoes.

The mixture was already beginning to bubble.

On February 21, with almost everyone objecting to one aspect or another, Dr. Euwe announced that new consultations would be held the following month in Moscow. He flew to the Russian capital at the beginning of March and, in a surprising concession, the Soviet Union agreed on March 4 to the original arrangement announced by Dr. Euwe. In a letter signed by the director of the Central Chess Club of the Soviet Union and handed to Dr. Euwe, the Russians accepted the split-site proposal and asked that meetings be held with chess representatives from the United States, Yugoslavia and Iceland to work out the details.

The details were announced on March 20. The prize money would be, as Dr. Euwe had said, $138,500 and, in the event of a 12–12 tie—which would entitle Spassky to retain his title—it would be split 50–50. Play was to begin in Belgrade on June 22, with three games a week scheduled and the 12th game to be played in Belgrade on July 18. The match would then switch to Iceland, and, if it went the full 24 games, the final game would be played in Reykjavik on August 31.

All seemed harmonious—until Fischer notified the tournament sponsors in Belgrade and Reykjavik that he wanted not only a share of the purse but also part of the profits from the tournament. And, said Fischer, he would negotiate himself, not through Colonel Edmondson.

FIDE, in turn, notified the United States Chess Federation that unless Fischer agreed to guarantee his appearance at the match under the stipulated financial arrangements, he would be disqualified as the challenger for the world title.

Fischer, who had been for some time in seclusion—as well as in training—at Grossinger's, the Catskill resort hotel favored by boxers, offered no guarantee. And FIDE issued no excommunicatory decrees. But it did set a deadline for Fischer (there would eventually be more deadlines set for the match than are met by a busy afternoon daily). If Fischer did not agree by midnight, April 4, to abide by the rulings of Dr. Euwe and to play under the conditions set forth, FIDE said, he could count himself out.

Fischer yielded. In a cablegram received at FIDE headquarters moments before the deadline, he said he was ready to play on the terms set forth by the international organization.

Nevertheless, he had made waves, and they broke on the shores of Yugoslavia. Chess officials there, perhaps remembering Fischer's past erratic behavior, his demands, his protests and his unceremonious exits from previous contests, demanded that the United States Chess Federation put up $35,000 to guarantee the challenger's appearance.

The request was relayed in a cablegram sent from Amsterdam by FIDE's secretary, H. J. J. Slavekoorte, to the United States group's offices in Newburgh, N. Y. John Hudson, administrative director of the American federation, said the organization didn't have that kind of money and didn't have any way to raise it. But, he added, the federation would go out in search of a benefactor.

A similar request was made to the Soviet Chess Federation and, on April 8, it said it was willing to put up the money. Unlike the U.S.C.F., which is a non-profit, non-governmental, volunteer group, the Soviet organization has the financial resources of the state at its disposal. Not only was it willing to put up the money, it also was able.

Fischer, in his just-under-the-deadline cable of acceptance, had said he was willing to abide by the rules set forth by FIDE. In a second cable from the Yugoslav sponsors received at Newburgh, the Yugoslavs asked whether this also meant that Fischer was willing to go along with the financial arrangements.

Whatever the answer, it didn't matter, for Colonel Edmondson, speaking for the United States Chess Federation, rejected the request for a $35,000 cash guarantee. "The guarantee was illegal," he explained later, because it was not provided for in any international chess regulations or in any of the agreements made for the match and because it "denied the rights of the challenger."

A few days later Yugoslav chess officials said they no longer wanted any part of the championship match.

The next step, Colonel Edmondson said, "is further negotiations," and he took that next step immediately, telephoning Dr. Euwe, who was in Australia on a lecture tour. Dr. Euwe, Colonel Edmondson said, "assured me that he would make every effort to save the situation." Dr. Euwe had already made strenuous efforts to keep the match alive and he would do so again—and be sharply rebuked for his troubles. The peacemaker's lot was not a happy one.

Behind the Yugoslavs' decision, Colonel Edmondson said, lay a misunderstanding caused by the FIDE secretariat's "being used to relay messages rather than having direct contact between the Belgrade organizers and the players."

At that point it looked hopeless. Belgrade was out and, with it, the first half of the match. How could there be a second half without a first? A search for a new site and new sponsors for the first half began.

On April 14, Dr. Euwe, still in Australia, cabled Slavekoorte in Amsterdam to institute an active search for a new first-half site. There was, he said, no time to seek new bids, and the host would have to be selected on a first-come, first-served basis.

"Whichever country can agree first to stage the match on conditions which have been arranged can have it straight away," he said.

Time was short, he added, because the match would have to end before the scheduled start of the World Chess Olympiad in Skopje, Yugoslavia, on September 18. "The new host will not have much time to complete the arrangements," he warned.

As for replacing the challenger instead of the site, Dr. Euwe said that was out of the question. "Fischer is the challenger," he said, "and he must have his chance. But it was his fault that the arrangements for Belgrade fell through, and I feel he should accept any new arrangements."

In a kind of wistful aside, the beleaguered chess official said he hoped The Netherlands, his homeland, would find the will and the money to become the host.

That was not to be. The next day, Wim Ruth, chairman of the Dutch Chess Union, said it was highly unlikely that his organization could raise the prize money. He blamed Fischer's "financial chicanery" for the sad state of the match arrangements and said "convincing sponsors to raise the necessary prize money seems an impossible task."

In the next few days, Paris, Puerto Rico and Australia cxpressed willingness to offer a venue for the match, but for one reason or another nonc of the offers bore fruit.

Iceland, already the site of the second half for which there still was no first half, then offered to be host to the entire match, at its original bid of $125,000 in prize money. FIDE, tired of trying to tie a neat bow with the tangled skein it had in hand, agreed. So did the Soviet Union—Reykjavik, after all, had been Spassky's first choice.

FIDE gave Fischer another deadline—May 6—to accept Reykjavik or find himself an ex-challenger. If he failed to respond, and to respond with an acceptance, he would be replaced, FIDE said, by Petrosian.

On May 5 Fischer agreed to play Spassky in Reykjavik "or anywhere else in the free world." But he did so under protest. Paul G. Marshall, one of his lawyers, said Fischer had agreed "in spite of the continued attempts by the Russian government to defend a title by chicanery instead of skill."

The site of the match, Fischer said (according to his lawyer), should have been chosen in a face-to-face meeting between himself and Spassky, but was not done this way because the Soviet government would not permit such a meeting or allow Spassky to travel freely. Not only that, said Fischer—still speaking through his lawyer—but FIDE was "biased" against him.

As for Iceland, said the lawyer, "while Mr. Fischer expressed admiration for both the people and the country, he noted that the lack of technical facilities there made televised coverage very difficult and severely hampered films or tape recordings of the event."

Fischer's chief aim, said the statement, "was to see that his friends in the Americas could for the first time see their representative play for the world championship."

That whole statement—that Iceland lacked facilities for TV coverage and that Fischer wanted his fellow Americans to be able to follow his fortunes on their home screens—was later to take on an ironic ring. But meanwhile the protests and demands continued, despite Fischer's agreement, and the publicity continued to increase in extent and intensity. Bit by bit, item by item, broadcast by broadcast, attention was being focused, if not on chess in general, then certainly on the world championship match, and on Fischer in particular.

Reykjavik was willing. Spassky was willing. Fischer was willing. The date was set: The first game was to be played on Sunday, July 2, at 5 P.M. Iceland time (1 P.M. Eastern Daylight Time). Games were to be played on Tuesdays, Thursdays and Sundays, with Wednesdays, Fridays and Mondays devoted, if necessary, to the playing-off of games unfinished the day before. Saturdays, in accordance with Fischer's standing wishes, were to be free. He is a member of a fundamentalist sect called the Worldwide Church of God, which, like Jews, observes the sabbath from sundown Fridays to sundown Saturdays. Fischer goes into seclusion for the sabbath.

The opening ceremonies, complete with welcoming speeches by the President of Iceland, the Lord Mayor of Reykjavik and others, were to be held on Saturday night, July 1, in the National Theater. The Russian Ambassador, the American Chargé d'Affaires and other members of the diplomatic corps were to be there, along —of course—with the champion, the challenger and their seconds and assistants.

On June 21, almost two weeks before the scheduled start of the match, Spassky and his entourage of three arrived in Reykjavik. There was Yefim Geller, one of the Soviet Union's strongest grandmasters and the officially designated second for the champion—the man who would sit up all night with him (or for him), analyzing adjourned positions and helping to work out the best lines of play. There was Nikolai Krogius, who was not only an international grandmaster, but also a practicing psychologist and a close friend of Spassky's. His duty would be to help bolster Spassky's nerves and attitude and to lift him, if needed, out of any fits of depression. And then there was Ivo Nei, an international master who would jog beside Spassky and play tennis with him—tennis is Spassky's favorite sport—to help keep him physically fit for the gruelling contest.

The champion and his retinue settled in, giving

themselves plenty of time to let their biological clocks adjust to the new time zone (and to the lack of darkness in a city that lies just below the Arctic Circle, where, in midsummer, the sun never sets). Spassky played tennis, jogged, slept and studied, relaxing while keeping himself in trim for the coming battle.

And Fischer? He had vanished.

Always hostile toward and suspicious of newsmen, the American grandmaster now was avoiding them more determinedly than ever. He left Grossinger's, where he had been working out like a prizefighter getting ready for the big one, and—it was believed—went to the West Coast. From time to time he would be heard from, usually through a spokesman, and what was heard were demands for a bigger piece of the action. In addition to the agreed-upon share of the record-breaking purse (the winner was to get $78,125, the loser $46,875) and 30 percent of the proceeds from television and film rights, Fischer wanted 30 percent of the box-office receipts.

As game time approached and Fischer failed to show up—or even to reveal his hiding place—the "war of nerves" theory surfaced and made the rounds. Fischer, according to this theory, was not just being his usual petulant, finicky, eccentric self; he was playing a game of psychological warfare with Spassky, and his demands, his protests, his disappearance—all were calculated to unnerve the supposedly unflappable Russian.

Spassky and Fischer had clashed over the chess board five times (the last time in 1970) and the results had been three victories for Spassky and two draws. The war-of-nerves theorists pointed to this record to help bolster their argument.

On June 25, without explanation, Fischer canceled his reservations on a flight to Reykjavik from Kennedy International Airport. Marshall, his lawyer, said that some detailed "ground rules" for the match had still to be worked out but that he did not expect this unfinished business to prevent Fischer from arriving in plenty of time for the July 2 start. Colonel Edmondson, too, expressed confidence that Fischer would show up on schedule.

The following day, Fred Cramer, a vice president of FIDE and a spokesman for Fischer, arrived in Iceland and indicated that Fischer would turn up later in the week. But that did little to satisfy either the curiosity of chess-watchers—who didn't even know where Fischer was—or the misgivings of the sponsors of the match, scheduled to be played in the 2,300-seat Exhibition Hall. The sponsors, who had gone to considerable expense to install special lighting and other equipment, were understandably nervous. Fischer's failures to show up and his hasty exits—they may well have remembered that he walked out in the middle of the elimination tournament in Tunisia in 1967 even though he was in first place at the time—were not easily forgotten.

Cramer, a lighting engineer from Minneapolis, was observed, shortly after his arrival, in Exhibition Hall with a light meter in his hand (Fischer had on occasion refused to play because lighting conditions were not to his liking). He was also seen looking over the rooms set aside for Fischer at the Loftleidir Hotel (Fischer is finicky about his accommodations and, during the match with Petrosian in Buenos Aires, had changed rooms at least three times in three days).

On the day of Cramer's arrival, Spassky granted a public interview at the Saga Hotel before a group of journalists (the champion holds a degree in journalism). A handsome, medium-sized man with thick brown hair, blue-green eyes and the figure of an athlete, he parried most of the questions with diplomatic tact.

Fischer, he said, has a playing style that is "very practical, with immense energy." He compared that style to Capablanca's and said he believed Fischer's playing had become "much stronger" since their last encounter.

Asked if he thought Fischer was conducting a war of nerves, he replied: "I think Fischer is the commander-in-chief of his own ideas."

As for how he would counter Fischer's all-but-inevitable opening move—pawn to king four—he grinned and said: "That is a professional secret."

Yes, he said, he always liked Iceland. No, he

hadn't seen the hall yet, but he was sure everything would be just fine.

It had been reported, one newsman said, that Spassky was demanding a room temperaure of 21 degrees Centigrade (about 70 degrees Fahrenheit), while Fischer was insisting on 24 degrees. How would the champion deal with that?

"I haven't asked for 21 degrees," he replied in characteristically amiable fashion, "but if there is a problem we can add 21 and 24 and divide by two."

Spassky avoided politics, though he did say, when pressed, that he was not a member of the Communist Party. He dismissed the widely held belief that the match was going to be an East-West confrontation. "While seated at the chess board," he said, "I am a chess player and not a politician."

While newsmen were interviewing the friendly and open Spassky in Reykjavik, others were trying vainly to discover Fischer's hiding place in the United States. He was, it was thought, somewhere in Queens, probably at the home of Fred M. Saidy in Douglaston. Saidy's son, Anthony Saidy, is a physician, a chess master and a friend of Fischer's. But inquiries at the Saidy home, and a reporters' stakeout there, led nowhere.

Then, on Thursday, June 29, Fischer was spotted in a restaurant at Kennedy Airport with his other lawyer, Andrew Davis, apparently waiting for an Icelandic Airlines flight to Reykjavik. As soon as Fischer saw the reporters and photographers he bolted from the restaurant, eluded his pursuers and vanished once more. Davis went on alone to Iceland.

Two days later, on July 1—the day planned for the welcoming ceremonies and one day before the scheduled start of the match—it was learned that Fischer, through Davis, had asked for a two-day postponement. Davis, in a meeting with officials of the Icelandic Chess Federation, the referee, Lothar Schmid of Germany, Dr. Euwe and Cramer, had pleaded that Fischer was too fatigued to play and thus not medically fit. (Under FIDE rules, a postponement can be granted to a player if he submits a certificate from an official doctor attesting to the need for the postponement.

Three such medical postponements are permitted each player during a match.)

This move only reinforced the war-of-nerves theory. But if there was psychological warfare going on, Spassky seemed to have escaped its effects. At lunch, he was seen laughing, joking and apparently relaxed and in the best of spirits.

That night, despite Fischer's absence, the opening ceremonies were held in the National Theater in Reykjavik. Some of the dignitaries who were supposed to have been there or to have participated either failed to show up or took no part if they did. And the atmosphere that had been expected to be festive was heavy indeed.

At Exhibition Hall, all was in readiness. Special heavy chairs had been brought in to help maintain the mausoleum-like silence so dear to chess competitors, and especially to Fischer. The 300-pound mahogany table built especially for the occasion (and meant to be deposited in a museum once the match was over) sat on the thickly carpeted stage. On the custom-built marble-inlay board stood the 32 hand-carved John Jacques & Son chess pieces that had been flown in from England. Everything was ready except the challenger.

In his negotiations, Davis proposed that Fischer make an appearance the following day but that, instead of playing, he participate only in a drawing for the right to play White (and thus have the first move) in the first game. In return for this postponement, Davis said, the United States delegation was prepared to offer the Russians an extra medical postponement.

The Russians said nothing, neither accepting nor rejecting Davis's proposals.

The day of the first game arrived with Fischer nowhere in sight, either in Reykjavik or New York.

Dr. Euwe, who had been in Iceland for some time trying desperately to shore up the apparently crumbling arrangements, granted Fischer a two-day postponement with the warning that, if he failed to show up in Reykjavik by noon Tuesday, July 4, he would forfeit the match.

"I think," the FIDE head said gloomily, "there will be no play at all."

And Spassky, informed at the breakfast table that Fischer was still somewhere in New York, looked shocked and said: "This is bad for chess."

Though there was no official reaction from the Soviet delegation, Spassky was quoted as saying that he had waited this long and that, out of deference to his Icelandic hosts, he could wait two days more for the match to begin.

But despite Spassky's willingness to bend and Dr. Euwe's granting of the two-day delay, some sticky problems were arising. The Russians, for example, were saying that the match officially started with the opening-night ceremonies and that Spassky would be the automatic winner if Fischer were disqualified. Thus, they said, the champion would be entitled to demand his five-eighths share of the purse and Fischer would be entitled to nothing.

The Americans contended, on the other hand, that the match would not officially start until the clock that times the players had been started and the first move had been made in the game.

Dr. Euwe's position was that there was nothing in the rules to cover the case; no player had ever been disqualified for failing to appear for a championship match.

There was also the possibility that the Icelandic Chess Federation would sue Fischer. Though Fischer had never signed a contract—he dislikes signing anything—he had sent a telegram to FIDE saying he would play the match in Iceland, under protest. That telegram, Dr. Euwe said he had been advised, would constitute legal acceptance.

The Icelandic Chess Federation stood to lose about $75,000 if the match were called off. Presumably, it would sue for that much plus punitive damages.

If Fischer were disqualified, Dr. Euwe said, there would be no further sanctions against him. He would not be barred from future matches or tournaments (though he might, of course, have trouble convincing anyone to underwrite a tournament or match in which he was scheduled to participate) and could, if he wished, compete in the next round of eliminations for the championship.

As far as he knew, the FIDE president said, Fischer was still somewhere in New York because he was unhappy about the financial arrangements. This was confirmed by a friend of Fischer's who spoke to him by phone and who said: "Bobby sounded calm and reasonable. His demands are entirely financial."

Meanwhile, efforts to salvage the match were still going on. Davis was still trying to work out a deal with the Icelandic federation and Fischer's friends—those who knew where he was—were phoning him, urging him to play. An Icelandic chess player named Freysteinn Thorbergsson who said he was a close friend of Fischer's flew to New York to try face-to-face persuasion.

Cramer, too, was busy. He said that two telegrams had been sent from New York to the Icelandic Chess Federation but had been lost. One of these, he said, was from the United States Chess Federation and was a request for a postponement of the match; the other was a doctor's statement (he declined to name the doctor).

Dr. Euwe and Schmid, the referee, said they had seen no telegrams and, in any case, Dr. Euwe added, an unsupported message from a doctor was meaningless and could not be interpreted as an official request for a medical postponement.

Over at Exhibition Hall, several hundred people showed up, unaware that the on-again, off-again match was, at that point, in the off-again stage.

And at the Saidy home in Queens, a man who declined to identify himself told a reporter that Fischer "was here until 48 hours ago." He would not say where Fischer had gone.

Thus passed the day on which the match was supposed to have started. Fischer remained out of sight and the status of the most talked-about, most publicized, most expensive and highest-prized chess event in history remained, at best, clouded. The first American since Frank Marshall to compete for the world crown, and the first to reach the penultimate step of the championship ladder since the Soviet Union captured the title in 1948, had until noon on Independence Day to show up in Iceland.

On the following day, Fischer came out of hiding —he had, indeed, been in the Saidy home—broke his silence and flew to Iceland, all within hours after a chess-playing British millionaire offered $125,000 to double the already unheard-of purse.

Fischer, meeting newsmen at the Saidy home, said that while he had not studied the offer, made by the investment banker James D. Slater, in detail, he had decided to go on with match because "there's an awful lot of prestige of the country at stake."

"We've had these problems with the organizations," he said. "They've been very petty, but it doesn't pay to be petty like they are."

Asked—and newsmen had been trying for weeks to get to Fischer to ask him this one—whether he was indeed conducting psychological warfare against Spassky, Fischer replied: "I don't believe in psychology; I believe in good moves."

Fischer, according to his lawyer Marshall, received word of the Slater offer at 8 A.M. New York time on July 3 and took about six hours to come to a decision. Marshall said Fischer's first reaction had been "I've got to accept it—it's stupendous." His only negative comment, said the lawyer, was that he felt "the English were assuming an Icelandic responsibility."

Slater, the 43-year-old chairman of Slater Walker Securities—which is said to control more than 250 companies around the world—has a personal fortune estimated at more than $6 million. His offer was first made in a telephone call to Dr. Euwe by Leonard Barden, a former British chess champion. Barden said he also had been in touch with Marshall several times during the day.

The offer was couched in a way that made refusal difficult. It said:

"If he isn't afraid of Spassky, then I, Jim Slater, have removed the element of money."

Fischer, said Marshall, had to accept because "he couldn't go down as a coward."

"This money is mine," Slater said. "I like chess and have played it for years. Many want to see this match and everything has been arranged. If Fischer does not go to Iceland, many will be disappointed."

And a spokesman for Slater added: "This puts Fischer behind the eight-ball. He will have to come out and play or show he is chicken."

Though the $125,000 offer accomplished what months of dickering, threatening and bargaining had failed to accomplish, Marshall insisted that the issue with Fischer had never been money.

"It was the principle," he said. "He felt Iceland wasn't treating this match or his countrymen with the dignity that it and they deserved. He was furious about the press censorship. He was flying around the room."

The "press censorship" of which Marshall spoke was a demand by the Icelandic Chess Federation that newsmen file not more than three dispatches during any one game.

"They're trying to stop America from reading about it," Marshall quoted Fischer as having said. "That's what they've done all along."

Whatever the reasoning—whether it was the challenge inherent in Slater's statement that he had removed "the problem of money," the lure of the money itself, the rapidly approaching deadline set by Dr. Euwe, or a combination of these elements—Fischer accepted. He left the Saidy home with three friends, and drove by back roads to Kennedy International Airport. There, in an isolated section, he transferred to an Icelandic Airlines station wagon and, at 9 P.M. on July 3, was in effect smuggled aboard a jetliner. The flight, scheduled for 7:30 P.M., took off at 10:04, which would get it to Reykjavik at 7 A.M., five hours before the deadline and ten hours before the rescheduled start of the first game.

But if the sky was clearing in New York, it was clouding over in Reykjavik. The Soviet Chess Federation lodged a "strong protest" from Moscow against the

48-hour postponement granted by Dr. Euwe and it said that Fischer's behavior warranted his "unconditional disqualification" from the match. The Soviet chess group charged that Dr. Euwe had acted without an official request from Fischer for a delay and it added that it would consider the match "wrecked" if Fischer once more failed to meet a deadline.

Spassky himself released a short statement that seemed to leave open a variety of options. It said:

"As I have heard that I have given permission to delay the beginning of the first game for two days, I want to declare that I have not given any such permission, not to the president of FIDE, not to anybody else. All talks about such permission from me therefore do not reflect reality."

In Newburgh, at the headquarters of the United States Chess Federation, Colonel Edmondson defended Fischer and said that Slater's doubling of the purse "means chess at last achieves the place in the sun that many people feel it deserves" and that "whatever else one may think of Bobby Fischer or his recent actions, he deserves the credit for it."

"He is a chess professional in a country which does not provide government support for chess players," the U.S.C.F. head continued, "and he should not be condemned for seeking the maximum private income for his endeavors."

Shortly before 7 A.M. Iceland time the jet touched down. Bobby Fischer, the center of more attention than had ever before been given to a chess player, the subject of controversy and contention and the object of adulation and animosity, slipped off to his room and went to sleep.

4 Personalities

The two men whose talent, skill and ambitions had brought them together on an all-but-treeless volcanic island midway between Moscow and New York were as different from each other in background and temperament as that subarctic island is from their birthplaces.

"You will understand Spassky better," a Soviet chess fan once said, "if you know that his favorite writer is Dostoyevsky and his favorite composer is Scriabin," the turn-of-the-century Russian metaphysical romantic.

If Fischer has a favorite composer, only he knows who that is; he does, however, listen to rock. And a favorite author? He has been seen reading *Playboy* when he is not deep in a chess journal (he knows enough Russian to be able to make his way through the Soviet chess publications, and he has a chess-knowledge of other languages).

Boris Vasilyevich Spassky was born in Leningrad on January 30, 1937, to a Russian father and a Jewish mother—in the Soviet Union, Jews, like Ukrainians or Latvians, are considered a separate nationality.

In 1941, during World War II, he and his older brother were evacuated and sent to an orphanage in the Kirov region. There he picked up the rudiments of chess by watching older boys play the game. At 6 he moved with his parents and brother to the outskirts of Moscow, where the family remained until its return to Leningrad after the war, in 1946.

Back in his home town, the young boy started going to meetings of the chess club in the city's Palace of Youth and he soon came under the tutelage of Vladimir G. Sak. Although he was considered a chess prodigy, Spassky was not allowed to become a one-sided prodigy. Sak did more than teach him chess; he selected books for the young boy, took him to the theater and got him involved in sports.

At 10, Spassky played in his first major event on

a chess tour that took him to the Crimea. At 11 he reached the top rank at the Youth Palace chess club and began collaborating with Alexander Tolusch, one of the Soviet Union's strongest players. In 1953, at an international competition in Bucharest, Spassky tied for 4th to 6th place (Tolusch won the tournament) and became an international master—at 16, the youngest Soviet player ever to attain that rating.

Since then Spassky's life has been a life of chess, a life studded with sparkling victories but marred as well by dismal failures—often at crucial moments. For the record, he is a journalist, holding a diploma from the journalism faculty of Leningrad University and a post as editor of the weekly chess magazine "64."

Though he has said publicly that he would just as soon relinquish the championship and return to a more relaxed way of life with his wife and son, Spassky is a fierce competitor whose record speaks eloquently of his driving ambition.

In 1955 he qualified for a place in the annual Soviet championship tournament in Moscow. In that tournament (which, like the U. S. championship, was considered a regional event in the world championship preliminaries) he placed in a tie for 3d to 6th place, just half a point below the winners, Vasily Smyslov and Geller, and he thus went on to the Interzonal.

At the Interzonal, which took place in the summer of '55 in Goteborg, Sweden, he was among the finishers, which not only sent him on to the candidates' competition, but also brought him the rank of grandmaster. He was 18 years old, the world junior champion, and the youngest Soviet chess player ever to become a grandmaster.

In the candidates' tournament (the rules had not yet been changed to make the candidates' event a knockout match instead of a round-robin tournament) Spassky again tied for a runner-up spot, this time 3d to 7th place, 2 points below the winner, Smyslov. He was out of the running for the world championship, but he had added new luster to a record that was already brilliant, and—even more important—he had picked up meaningful new experiences in the difficult, grueling world of competition chess.

For the next few years Spassky had his moments of glory, winning tournaments and titles, and his moments of despair, when the titles eluded him, often by heartbreakingly slim margins.

One of those moments of despair came in 1958, during the preliminaries for the world title match. He was paired with Mikhail Tal—Tal the Terrible—a former world champion whose often brilliant, sometimes erratic, never dull style had made him something of a glamorous star in the chess firmament. (Tal's style and even, to an extent, his personality, have been compared to Fischer's from time to time. In recent years, his ill health has kept him away from active competition.)

In a crucial game in the final round, Spassky conjured up a brilliant attack that, by all rights, should have crushed Tal. But he blundered away his advantage and lost the game. His outward calm dissolved, and he wept openly and unashamedly.

Spassky had to watch the world championship contest from the sidelines.

Three years later, in 1961, Spassky again slipped at a critical moment and once more had to play the role of observer as the world title competition was played out.

Spassky had learned chess at first by playing, not by reading theoretical works or studying the games of the masters. All that had changed when he entered the dead-serious world of competition. Now, once more, Spassky changed, and he focused his intellectual and emotional faculties on his objective: the world championship.

At the next zonal tournament, held in Moscow early in 1964, Spassky, despite his efforts, began by taking only one point in the first four rounds. But his ability to remain calm in the face of adversity helped to pull him through. He rallied and, by the time the last round was over, he was in first place.

The Interzonal that followed in Amsterdam later in the year ended in a four-way tie for first place among Spassky, Smyslov, Tal and Larsen.

Then came the candidates' playoffs. Spassky picked off the competition with ease, defeating Paul Keres 6 to 4, Geller 5½ to 2½ and, finally, Tal the Terrible, 7 to 4. Only Petrosian stood between him and the world championship.

Petrosian proved to be a powerful barrier, and Spassky once more found himself short of his goal by a slim margin; he lost the championship match 11½ to 12½.

Seeded into the next candidates' playoffs, Spassky overcame first Geller, 5½ to 2½, then Larsen, 5½ to 2½ and, finally, Korchnoi, 6½ to 3½. And then, once more, came Petrosian.

This time, after 23 rounds, Spassky had what he had always wanted—the world championship.

Under the old rules, Petrosian could have challenged him for a return match the following year, in 1970. But the rules had been changed and Spassky could now enjoy his title for three unthreatening years, while others fought for the right to challenge him.

The man who won that right was born Robert James Fischer on March 9, 1943, in Chicago. Like Spassky, one of his parents—his father—was Jewish. When he was 2, his parents were divorced and Fischer and his older sister, Joan, were taken by their mother to Brooklyn. To keep her little brother amused, Joan Fischer bought a chess set and taught him the moves.

Teaching the 6-year-old Bobby Fischer to play chess must have been, in a way, like teaching the baby Mozart to play the clavier. The combination was immediate, electric, cataclysmic.

The little boy began haunting the Brooklyn Chess Club, the same one at which the American grandmaster Frank J. Marshall had made his debut. It was there that he suffered one of his early defeats, in a simultaneous exhibition, by Max Pavey when he was 8 years old.

Though he tended to burst into tears when he lost in those days, he also did something that other preteenage boys did not do: he plunged head first into the vast sea of chess books, determined to become stronger than any of his opponents.

In later years Fischer was to say he never memorized variations and lines. Perhaps, in the sense that he may not deliberately set out to memorize, this is true. But it is also true that he never forgets a game he has played, or one that his opponent has played. When he sees an analysis it seems to become indelibly impressed on his brain.

By the time he was 10, Fischer had already started playing in tournaments, where his talents became obvious—especially to those who had to face the skinny kid across the chessboard.

When he was 12, Fischer became a member of the Manhattan Chess Club, one of the strongest in the world. He would wander into the club with a copy of a Russian chess magazine sticking out of one pocket, a copy of a Spanish chess periodical sticking out of another, an American or British publication clutched in his hand.

At the club he was dead serious. He played then—as he plays now—to win, and each game was a life-and-death thing.

He was 13 when he won the U. S. Junior Open (the tournament is open to anyone under 20, and Fischer was the youngest ever to capture the title) and 14 when he won the U. S. championship.

The tournament that made Fischer the youngest United States champion in history was the Lessing Rosenwald Tournament. Held in New York City in 1957, it attracted Lombardy, Reshevsky, Arthur Bisguier and James Sherwin, among others—a tough, talented, experienced group of chess veterans.

Fischer swept the tournament with 10½ points out of a possible 13, a fantastic record even for a seasoned master, and an unbelievable one for a 14-year-old boy.

Fischer, along with the 2d- and 3d-place winners in the tournament, qualified for the Interzonal that was to be held in Yugoslavia the following year. The strongest chess players in the world were to be there, and Fischer—still trying to show the world his strength—was to be among them.

At the Interzonal, Fischer ended up in a tie for 5th-6th. This put him into the coming Candidates tournament and also made him, at 15, the youngest grandmaster in chess history.

His first shot at the championship stopped there. But he had come close, winning the Zonal, placing in the Interzonal, and making it to the Candidates, where he finished 5th-6th.

That candidates tournament, plus a tournament in Zurich in the summer of 1959 that attracted most of the soon-to-be candidates, helped to convince Fischer that the Russians had conjured up a conspiracy designed to keep the championship within the Soviet Union.

That idea—that the Russians were against the rest of the world in general (and against him in particular) —was to become a dominant one with Fischer for many years.

Left behind in the 1959 Candidates' tournament, Fischer had to bide his time for another crack at the world championship. His waiting time was not idle. He won the U. S. championship twice more, with the third championship victory, in 1960, qualifying him once again for the Interzonals and putting him, for the second time, on the road to the world title.

After blazing a brilliant path across a whole series of other tournaments and matches, Fischer went into the Interzonal confident of victory. He was right; he finished first—the first time the Interzonal had not been captured by a Soviet star—with a winning margin of 2½ points, not the kind of margin that goes with playing for draws.

At the Candidates tournament he lost three of his first five games. In the later rounds he closed the gap, but not enough, and he finished in 4th place. Thus ended his second attempt to seize the world championship.

It was after that candidates competition that Fischer said he would not compete again until the rules were changed to prevent collusion among the Soviet players.

Fischer did return to international competition, despite his threat, but his return ended with his walkout in Tunisia in 1967. The rest is recent history.

What is it that makes this gangling, adolescent-looking young man a phenomenon?

"All I want to do, ever, is play chess."

That just about sums up what makes Fischer different. He lives for one thing and one thing alone—chess.

He left Erasmus Hall High School in Brooklyn in his junior year because "the stuff they teach you in school I can't use one way or the other." Meaning, if it wasn't applicable to chess, it wasn't of any earthly use.

Spassky has an apartment in Moscow, a wife, a son. Fischer lives out of suitcases, calling whatever hotel or friend's home he is staying in at the moment his home. He has no wife, though he has said he might someday want to get married.

At 14 Fischer said he liked to see his opponents squirm. On television, shortly before the Spassky match, he amplified on that remark, saying the greatest moment in a game, for him, comes when his opponent drifts into a lost position "and I feel I can crush his ego."

For Fischer the world is divided into two kinds of people—good chess players and "hacks." No one else exists.

Chess, says Fischer "demands total concentration—yeah, and a love for the game."

Larry Evans says the thing that makes Fischer different from all other chess players is that he "has been willing to give up his personal life" for chess.

Fischer agrees, but adds: "They call me temperamental, but I'm not. I don't go out of my way to look for trouble."

Fischer, according to some of the psychiatrists who are regulars at the Manhattan Chess Club, is a paranoid and is "psychotically suspicious, like most paranoids." And this, in turn, they say, accounts for what others call his gall, or his conceit or his inflated sense of self.

Fischer, like most paranoids, they say, cannot lie. And when he says he is the greatest, he is only telling the truth as he sees it.

At 29, Fischer has become something of a living legend. Certainly he is the most famous chess player of the age, or possibly of any age. And by being that, by doing what he has been doing, he has brought a new sense of self, not only to himself, but to all other chess players as well.

Though the center stage was monopolized by the two principals, others were also on stage or in the wings. The organizers, the chess federation officials, the arbiters, the seconds and assistants and spokesmen—all helped keep the play moving even when the main actors had no lines or action.

The most conspicuous of the supporting players, at least as far as the public in the hall was concerned, was Lothar Schmid, the referee.

Schmid was no newcomer to Fischer games; he had been the referee at the match with Petrosian in Buenos Aires. He had had to use his considerable powers of persuasion there on several occasions, including one in which Fischer had claimed a draw by repetition and Petrosian had contested it. Fischer, the referee explained to Petrosian, was correct.

But the problems of Buenos Aires were to pale beside those of Reykjavik. Dr. Euwe had put it succinctly when—after all the harrowing negotiations, postponements, protests, demands and other skirmishes—he had turned responsibility for the match over to Schmid.

"Now," Euwe said, "it is all yours."

And indeed it was. The 44-year-old German-born grandmaster was in full charge; he was the ultimate arbiter. Not even the International Chess Federation could step in, except under the most extraordinary circumstances.

"I have full responsibility for things that can happen on and off the stage," he said with a wry smile when he took over, knowing full well that as much off-stage as on-stage action might well be expected.

On-stage problems could include such issues as the touch move, for instance, when a player claims that his opponent has touched a piece and must therefore, under the formal rules, move it. The referee must decide who is right.

There is—as there was in Buenos Aires—the possibility of a claim of draw by repetition. Or the lights may go out (as, again, they did in Argentina) and the referee must stop both players' clocks.

Sometimes the disputes can border on the silly.

Fischer, for example, had objected in Buenos Aires to Petrosian's habit of writing the move on his score sheet and then making the move (most players move first and then write). Schmid urged Petrosian to reverse his normal procedure and Petrosian did.

It may well have been that Schmid's charm as much as Petrosian's good nature smoothed that one over, for the handsome, genial, easy-smiling Schmid can exercise a great deal of charm. One grandmaster tells of the time he played Schmid—who became a grandmaster in 1959—some years back:

"I think I had the edge," he said. "I was studying the position, then looked at Schmid. He gave me this great big smile of his and grabbed my hands. I agreed to the draw.

"It was the first and only time I have ever been charmed into a draw."

Born in Dresden, Schmid moved with his family to Bamberg after World War II and became a lawyer. But his great love was chess, and he spent much time with and at it.

He played on student teams, representing West Germany in international tournaments, then became an internationl master and a grandmaster. In recent years he has played relatively little and describes himself as an "amateur" whose profession is publishing—he is the head of the Karl May publishing house in Bamberg.

There are some grandmasters, however, who feel that publishing's gain was chess's loss, for they say that Schmid—had he gone on with chess as a profession—might well have been among the greats.

It might have been less of a strain, too, for Schmid, to be a player instead of a referee. His frequent pressing of the button that turned on the giant "SILENCE" sign in the playing hall, and his occasional strolls to the front of the stage to appeal by mute gesture to the audience to be quiet, failed to make an impression on Fischer, who at one point called Schmid "arrogant and inconsiderate" for not doing more to maintain silence in the hall.

If Schmid was the most visible of the supporting players, the others were no less important.

Lombardy, for example, the Roman Catholic priest who was Fischer's second, played far more than a peripheral role. He had been among those who had helped, initially, to persuade Fischer to go to Reykjavik. And, once the match began, he functioned—as did others in the challenger's retinue—to keep the world away from Fischer.

Easy to talk to, quick to smile and laugh, a fast man with a pun or joke, Lombardy did not give the impression of seriousness so frequently associated with the priesthood or with grandmastership.

Nonetheless, he was serious in both.

When he won the world junior chess championship in 1957, he took all 11 of his games. He became a grandmaster in 1960, won the United States Open in 1963 and was a co-winner of the Open in 1965. Two years later he was ordained, and he has been rated as the strongest chess-playing clergyman since Ruy Lopez.

Long a close friend of Fischer, the 35-year-old Lombardy teaches English at Cardinal Hayes High School in the Bronx.

Lombardy's counterpart on the Russian side was Geller, and as a second for this match, nobody could have been better. A grandmaster since 1952 and champion of the U. S. S. R. in 1955, Geller had racked up more victories against Fischer than any other chess player, including Spassky and Tal. His job would be to help the champion analyze adjourned games—a job that could take all night.

The second also acts as the player's factotum—shielding him, seeing that he gets proper rest and good food, waking him when necessary, taking care of the myriad minor details with which the star should not be bothered if he is to concentrate all his time and energy on the task at hand, winning chess games. A good second also sees to it that the player's spirits are kept up in the face of setbacks. For Geller (and for Krogius and Nei) this was to turn out to be a full-time occupation.

5 The Confrontation

At last—after cancellations, protests, demands, disappearances—Bobby Fischer was in Reykjavik. He had arrived five hours before the deadline set for his disqualification and 10 hours before the so-often-rescheduled start of his by now notorious match with Boris Spassky.

But the game was not played that day. The collective sigh of relief that seemed to have been heard when Fischer's jet touched down in Iceland turned into a groan, because the match was postponed once more. But this time it was the Russians who were making demands.

Spassky had showed up at a meeting at which lots were to be drawn for the right to play White in the first game. But when he got there he found, not Fischer, but Lombardy, who had accompanied Fischer to Iceland to be his second. Fischer was said to be still fast asleep in his room.

Instead of going through with the ceremony, Spassky stalked out of the room. Later, Tass, the Soviet press agency, supplied a statement, in translation, that it said Spassky had made. It said:

"Fischer broke the rules of holding the contest by refusing to come for the ceremony of opening the match. By this Fischer insulted me, personally, and the Chess Federation of the U.S.S.R., which I represent.

"The public opinion in the U.S.S.R. and I, personally, are indignant over Fischer's conduct. Under all human notions, he discredited himself completely. By this he jeopardized his moral right to play in the match for the world chess crown.

"Fischer must bear the just punishment before there is a hope of holding the match. Only after this can I return to the question about the possibility of holding the match."

The Tass news story said: "Robert Fischer arrived today in Reykjavik but he did not appear at the conference by 12 o'clock, thus showing again his disrespect for all. Instead, an American wearing a clergyman's habit, whom no one saw in Reykjavik before, arrived in the hall and presented a written mandate from Fischer declaring that he will represent Fischer at the drawing of the lots. It was said that Fischer is now sleeping."

Neither Spassky nor the Soviet Chess Federation nor Tass gave any hints about what kind of "just punishment" would have to be meted out to Fischer to satisfy their wounded feelings and sense of outrage. But the champion did say that he had no intention of leaving Iceland. "I still want to play the match if there is a solution," he said, adding: "I will make my decision in the next few days."

While Fischer slept, his entourage busily tried to soothe ruffled feelings. But Dr. Euwe was still on the pessimistic side.

"The situation is critical," he said. "I don't know if the match will be played at all."

The 71-year-old FIDE chief, a tall, courtly man, also said he knew he was following "a correct middle course" because "first the Americans attacked me, and now the Russians."

The Soviet delegation had charged Dr. Euwe with committing procedural errors, bending the rules in Fischer's favor.

In New York, Colonel Edmondson said he did not think Spassky had acted on his own.

"I believe," he said, "that he is acting under the orders of the Soviet Chess Federation. I have always found Spassky to be a gentleman and a good sport. And the action of the Soviet Chess Federation shows the true color of their sportsmanship.

"On Sunday, when it appeared that Bobby Fischer might not go to Iceland, they did not object to the postponement of the match for two days as announced by Dr. Euwe. But now that Fischer is in Iceland, prepared to play, the Soviets are showing their true colors by instructing Spassky to obstruct the match.

"As a [FIDE] Bureau member, it is my opinion that this charade has gone far enough. Fischer's actions, though some of us may not think he went about it in the best manner, have been quite logical. He achieved his goal when the very generous gentleman from England doubled the prize fund.

"The entire charade should end. I recommend that the FIDE president establish a firm starting date, preferably this Thursday [July 6] and forfeit either player if he doesn't show. And I make this recommendation because I consider the present Soviet objections to be insincere and merely an attempt at a psychological ploy against Fischer. My personal opinion is that they've made a tactical error by not playing today. Spassky has given Fischer two days in which to physically recover from the fatigue brought on by his overnight flight from New York City and four-hour change in time zone."

That evening, Lombardy—who, with Paul Marshall, the lawyer, had conferred all day with the Russians, said that the negotiation, though delicate, were proceeding on a friendly basis. Another meeting had been scheduled for the following day, he said, and he hoped that the issues could at that time be resolved to everyone's satisfaction.

Several grandmasters, in discussing the Russian tactic, came to a number of differing conclusions. One school of thought held that Spassky should have demanded a game at once, before Fischer's biological clock had a chance to adjust. Others said Spassky was too angry to play his best game and had moved correctly—from a tactical point of view—in refusing to play. Spassky, these experts said, is more of an attacking player than the precise Fischer, and in his eagerness to punish the American might have launched an unsound and suicidal attack.

If there is any one word to characterize the day that followed, it is "confusion." Fischer tendered an apology that was addressed to the Soviet delegation. It said:

"We are sorry that the world championship was delayed. The problems causing the delays were not with world champion Spassky, whom I respect and admire as a man and a player.

"If grandmaster Spassky or the Soviet people were inconvenienced or discomforted, I am indeed unhappy for I had not the slightest intention of this occurring."

The Russians angrily rejected the apology. For one thing, said Geller, Spassky's second, it was not signed. For another, it was mimeographed. And for a third it was sent by messenger, not delivered personally by Fischer.

Fischer still had not made a public appearance and, in fact, had not been seen since he got off the plane. Lombardy said that Fischer disliked signing anything and wanted to explain his side of the story personally to Spassky.

The Russians went beyond simply rejecting Fischer's mimeographed apology. They turned on Dr. Euwe and demanded that he condemn Fischer's behavior and that he admit that his own action in granting a two-day postponement had violated FIDE rules.

Dr. Euwe responded at a press conference. Looking agitated, he said that since two of the Russian demands involved him—the third was the demand for a written, hand-delivered apology from Fischer—he would take care of them then and there. He wrote out a condemnation of Fischer, saying the American had acted in an "inexcusable manner" and was "living in another world." And he condemned Fischer's late arrival and his behavior "not only in the last two days, but all through the negotiations."

He also signed a statement conceding that he had violated FIDE rules in granting the two-day postponement. But, he said, "there are reasons."

"If I had not violated the rules," he said, "there would be no match." And, he added, he had broken the rules "on the basis of assumptions proved wrong."

In what seemed designed to give everyone a chance to cool down, Dr. Euwe proposed, on the spur of the moment, that the match be postponed another week and that it be split, with six to eight games to be played in another city later in the year. Nothing came of that proposal.

The Russian demands, the condemnation of Fischer and the concession by Dr. Euwe were followed by new demands from the American side. Cramer, Fischer's spokesman, called a news conference and said that if there was any apologizing to be done, it should be done by Dr. Euwe—to the Americans. Dr. Euwe, Cramer said, had broken the rules not in favor of Fischer, but in favor of Spassky.

"Anyway," Cramer added, "Bobby doesn't feel he has violated any rules."

Cramer—who had once blurted out that as Fischer's spokesman he was "authorized only to complain and not to approve"—went on to say he would waive all apologies if the drawing for the white pieces took place that night. It did not.

As the evening wore on, a faint feeling of hope started to emerge. Dr. Euwe, the Russians, the referee and members of the Icelandic Chess Federation were still conferring, and there were reports that Dr. Euwe felt the major outstanding differences had been ironed out.

The only light note of the day came in an announcement from Moscow that a group of Americans was using a computer in New York to help Fischer. These Americans would, by means unexplained in the announcement, get the moves of each game as it was going on, feed them into a computer and relay back to Fischer—also by some mysterious method—the best moves, as the computer saw them.

The announcement brought hysterical laughter from the chess specialists gathered in Reykjavik, including the referee, Schmid. Even the Russians smiled at the "news" from Moscow.

"That's nonsense," said Schmid.

"Asinine. Pure fantasy," said Jack Collins, a former New York State champion.

"Ridiculous," commented Larry Evans, the former U. S. champion.

"Computers," said Dr. Euwe, "play average chess —very bad."

While all this was going on in Iceland, Russians in Russia were reacting too. One newspaper editor buttonholed an American at a reception and said indignantly: "It is a money-grubbing society like yours that produces a Bobby Fischer. If anything like this ever happened in the Soviet Union, the pressure of public opinion would never stand for it."

The editor, in condemning Fischer's emphasis on money, spoke in highly ideological terms, making no allowance for personal idiosyncrasies or eccentricities as possible factors. But even less ideologically oriented Russians accused Fischer of dragging the game of chess from the lofty esteem in which it is held in Russia to the level of betting on horses and other sports-gambling events.

Fischer, the first American since Van Cliburn to capture the imagination of the Russian people, and to become almost a folk-hero, was taking on a decidedly tarnished image.

But in Reykjavik, the faint feelings of optimism that had begun to emerge proved to be not without justification. The talks, which went on well into the night, bore fruit and, on July 6—after months of bickering and battling, after protests and postponements and frustrations—the world championship match formally got under way.

The sword that finally sliced through the Gordian knot was a handwritten and signed apology delivered from Fischer to Spassky.

Text of Fischer's Apology

Dear Boris,

Please accept my sincerest apology for my disrespectful behavior in not attending the opening ceremony. I simply became carried away by my petty dispute over money with the Icelandic chess organizers. I have offended you and your country, the Soviet Union, where chess has a prestigious position.

Also, I would like to apologize to Dr. Max Euwe, president of FIDE, to the match organizers in Iceland, to the thousands of chess fans around the world and especially to the millions of fans and the many friends I have in the United States.

After I did not show up for the first game, Dr. Euwe announced that the first game would be postponed without prejudice to me. At that time, you made no protest. Now I am informed that the Russian Chess Federation is demanding that the first game be forfeited to you. The timing of this demand seems to place in doubt the motives for your federation's not insisting at the first for a forfeit of the first game.

If this forfeit demand were respected, it would place me at a tremendous handicap. Even without this handicap, you will have an advantage to begin with of needing 12 points out of 24 to retain your title, whereas I will need 12.5 to win the world title.

If this demand were granted, you would need only 11 points out of 23 but I would still need 12.5 out of my 23. In other words, I must win three games without losses, just to obtain the position you would have at the beginning of the match and [I] don't believe that the world champion desires such an advantage in order to play me.

I know you to be a sportsman and a gentleman, and I am looking forward to some exciting chess games with you.

Sincerely,
BOBBY FISCHER

The demand for a forfeit mentioned in Fischer's note was dropped and, shortly after the apology was accepted, the match formally began with a ceremony at which Fischer and Spassky drew lots for the right to play White—and thus have the first move—in the first game. It was to be done in the time-honored way used by most chess players: One player takes a white piece in one hand and a black piece in the other, hides them behind his back and then presents his clenched fists to his opponent, who points to one of the fists. Point to a fist holding a white piece and you play White; point to one holding a black piece, and you play Black.

Spassky arrived precisely on time for the ceremony. Fischer was 20 minutes late. Both met backstage and then went onto the stage of Exhibition Hall for the draw. The referee offered each player an envelope. The one Spassky chose notified him that he would be the one to hide the pieces behind his back and then present his clenched fists to Fischer. He did so, and Fischer pointed to Spassky's right hand. The champion opened it to reveal a black pawn.

Fischer's face did not change expression.

Fischer would not use the chairs provided by the Icelandic Chess Federation. Instead, he would sit in a special chair flown in from New York—a duplicate of the chrome-and-leather swivel chair he used in his match in Buenos Aires against Petrosian.

The chessboard, too, was special. Made of inlaid marble by Icelandic artisans, it had too much glare at first, and acid was used to reduce the glare. Fischer had not yet made up his mind about it.

During the ceremony of the draw, various features of the hall were tested. Of primary interest was the screen above the stage, which had a close-up of the board. The definition was not everything it should have been. Much better was a diagramatic representation, with the clocks of the players on one side. This was designed to let the audience see how much time each player had used up. As in most formal chess events, the players would be required to make 40 moves each in two and a half hours—a total of five hours of playing time—and at the end of that time either player could call for adjournment of the unfinished game to the following day.

After the ceremony, Fischer and Spassky shook hands, looking at each other the way Joan Sutherland and Maria Callas might—not with love, perhaps, but with mutual respect. They were a study in contrasts: Fischer tall, lumbering, looking somewhat ill at ease; the shorter Spassky collected and smiling. It was a contrast that was, eventually, to reverse itself.

Fischer left the hall immediately after the formalities and went to Keflavik Airfield to bowl at the United States Air Force Base there.

Although the ceremony took place on a Thursday,

it was decided not to hold the first game on the following Sunday (though the playing schedule was Sundays, Tuesdays and Thursdays, with games to begin at 5 P.M. Iceland time). The first over-the-board moves were to be made on Tuesday, July 11, to give both men a chance to recover from the nervous strain of the preceding days.

During the day there was a threat from the American delegation that a Sunday game was mandatory. Fischer, the delegation said, was eager to play on Sunday, and it was with difficulty that he was persuaded to go along with the Tuesday opening. But that last hurdle was passed and—it seemed—all was over but the chess-playing.

The confrontations involving Fischer and Spassky had, quite rightly, been the center of attention. But that did not mean that other confrontations had not taken place. One of these involved television coverage—an issue that was to become even stickier in the coming weeks. And with a lull in the Fischer-Spassky battle (the battle of wills—and won'ts—had apparently ended and the battle of chessmen had not yet begun), the others came into public view.

The Icelandic Chess Federation, in what it said was an effort to recoup some of its costs (it had by now invested close to $200,000, including the $125,000 prize fund), had signed a contract granting exclusive film rights to Chester Fox, Inc., and an agreement to let the World Chess Network have all move-by-move broadcasts. To prevent others from staging play-by-play reconstructions of the match, the federation had asked newsmen to sign an agreement before receiving press credentials. The agreement—the one that Marshall said had infuriated Fischer—said:

"We hereby request permission for our duly authorized representative to attend the world chess championship matches between Boris Spassky and Bobby Fischer, which are to be staged in Reykjavik commencing on or about July 2, 1972.

"In return for your granting this license to us to cover the championship matches, we agree to be bound by the following limitations:

"1. Our reports will be news reports and will be used only for bona fide news purposes.

"2. Our reports will not be the basis for any re-creation, reproduction or other unauthorized use of the play-by-play of the match.

"3. We will only make three reports per game and each report will be at least five minutes after either player makes a move.

"This above document will be used and no reporters or news agencies will get press accreditation unless signing."

The proposal drew heated reactions from many of the more than 100 newsmen who had converged on Reykjavik. Photographers, in particular, protested when told they would not be allowed even to take cameras into the hall when the match was in progress.

Rekyjavik's leading newspaper, *Morgunbladid,* called the restrictions unconstitutional and said it would fight them. *The New York Times* instructed its reporters not to sign the agreement and to get into the hall by buying spectator tickets—they cost $5 each—instead of using press credentials. *The Times*'s position was that, although the ban had virtually no effect on its coverage, it constituted prior restraint on reporting.

In New York, WNET-TV, Channel 13, said it would go on the air, as it had planned to do, with whatever plays it could get and would provide analyses and comments by Shelby Lyman (the chess master who had introduced McCandlish Phillips to the mysteries of the game).

Eventually, the television and film dispute almost led again to a Fischerian walkout. But for the moment—in that interval between the draw for the first move and the first move itself—the dispute was only simmering, and it seemed to be the only disturbing element.

But as though to demonstrate that something always had to be threatening the match, Schmid received a message that his 10-year-old son had been hurt in a bicycle accident. He flew home to Germany. The injuries proved to be not serious, however, and Schmid returned to Reykjavik in time to be referee for the first game. Still, it seemed to be a sign, a reminder, that the match had not yet really begun, and that something could go awry at any time.

On July 10, the day before the opening game, Spassky was reported to be tense but confident and undergoing a last-minute bout of nervousness. Fischer was said to be relaxed and happy. Spassky played tennis in the morning, then disappeared from public view. Fischer, who had swum the night before, slept through most of the day, as he frequently did.

Lloyds of London had established odds, making Fischer an odds-on favorite.

Some work still remained to be done in Exhibition Hall. The Russian delegation visited it and found everything satisfactory except the chessboard. The glare had finally been adequately reduced—by making a new board—but the marble squares, 2⅝ inches on a side, were, the Russians said, too large in relation to the chess pieces. Fischer agreed.

The board was the third one made by Sigurdur Helgason, an artisan who made his living cutting gravestones when he was not making special chessboards for world championship matches. Helgason went to work on a new board, cutting light gray Italian marble and green slate into squares 2¼ inches on each side.

The board was not the only thing Fischer complained about. In his visit to the hall he also found the lighting not to his taste and the distance between the players' table and the audience too short. Electricians were called in to adjust the lighting and the distance between the edge of the players' table and the audience was measured. It came to 40 feet, exactly what Fischer's contract called for.

After a slack period brought on by the disputes and uncertainties surrounding the match, the Icelandic tourist bureau reported, on the eve of the first game, that there had been a "reasonable increase" in tourism. Ticket sales for the match had dropped off, too, because of the problems, and the hall was not expected to scheduled start—July 2—now found themselves run-
be even half filled for the start the next day.

Many visitors who had shown up for the originally ning out of time, without having seen a move. There was a good deal of grumbling and unhappiness among them.

July 11, the great day, arrived at last. Despite the pessimistic predictions of some people, the hall was almost filled. There were more than 2,000 in the audience. They had started showing up well over an hour before the scheduled 5 P.M. opening, hoping to get the best seats.

The champion walked onto the stage promptly at 5, wearing a dark business suit with a vest. He spoke briefly to the referee, then made his first move—P-Q4 The referee started Fischer's clock, and he and Spassky waited. Seven minutes later, Fischer, wearing a business suit and white shirt, showed up. He studied the board a moment and made his first move—1 . . . N-KB3.

The game and the match were under way.

For most of the game there was hardly any movement by the players or the hushed audience in the dim arena. Fischer hunched over the board most of the time; Spassky had his head locked in his hands.

If the interior of the auditorium resembled a place of worship—from time to time a large "silence" sign would blink on—the exteriors were more reminiscent of Yankee Stadium at the seventh-inning stretch. Even hot dogs were on sale. Hundreds of fans gathered in the cafeteria of the hall and watched the action over television monitors installed there, pocket chess sets in front of them. They would work out variations while drinking beer or eating some of the calorie-sensational pastries that Icelanders love.

Downstairs there was a lecture room in which experts presided over a demonstration set hung on the wall. The room was jammed with chess fans jostling each other and even standing on chairs to see and hear the analysis. In sharp contrast to the immobility and silence in the playing arena itself, the halls and passageways were filled with noise and motion.

All the demonstration equipment worked beautifully. The closed-circuit television concentrated mostly on a demonstration board that, of course, kept up with the players' moves. Next to this were duplicates of the players' clocks, showing their elapsed time, and a complete list of the moves made thus far.

The television picture was sharp and clear. Every so often the camera would swing to the players, or to a close-up of the board itself, the new marble-and-slate board the artisans had worked so diligently to perfect. It had been installed shortly before game time and had met the approval of both players.

And the game? It began quietly enough, but, on the 29th move, it exploded. Spassky offered a pawn that, in the opinion of many experts, could not be taken; it was a "poisoned pawn." If Fischer snatched it, his bishop would probably be trapped.

Fischer did grab it—and gasps of surprise swept through the auditorium. Had Spassky miscalculated? Or had Fischer misjudged, giving up the bishop for two pawns and a tenuous position?

At adjournment the players retired to a night of analysis, testing lines of play arising from the complicated adjourned position. They were not alone. Virtually every chess player at the scene would be seeking variations, seeing if he or she could find the best line for Black or White. Though most grandmasters and experts gave the edge to Spassky, some still felt that Fischer had at least a chance to draw.

A night of analysis had convinced almost all the experts that Fischer's 29th move—his taking the "poisoned pawn"—had indeed been a lapse, and one of the strangest in grandmaster history. Spassky evidently had been one of those to come to that conclusion, for at breakfast he was seen smiling and looking confident and relaxed. Fischer was not to be seen at all.

Any number of theories were put forward to explain Fischer's move—his "blunder," as many called it. One, taken seriously by chess experts, involved the temperament of the players. Fischer, the thinking went, was so eager to win the first game that Spassky purposely played a dull line, trading off pieces and waiting for the bored and irritated challenger to do something rash. In short, according to this theory, Fischer was lured out of a draw into a lost position.

The theory may sound far-fetched, but such things had been known to happen. Larsen, the Dane Fischer routed on his way to the championship match, had been known to throw games away in his eagerness to win. Such impulsiveness was not normal to Fischer's cool, precise style, but that first game was something special, and Fischer might well have gambled—and lost.

Another theory held that Fischer had been so preoccupied with the business and other non-chess aspects of the match that he had not prepared himself as thoroughly as he might have.

And still another was not really a theory. It was simply a belief that the great Bobby Fischer had just made a mistake.

"Fischer did not think enough about the move," said one American grandmaster. "He rushed into it and he goofed."

There was a good-sized audience for the resumption of the first game, and it was as enthusiastic and well-behaved as it had been for the first part. Many had binoculars (one who had reported that Spassky's face had taken on a look of incredulity when Fischer had made that 29th move the night before).

If Fischer's 29th move was the highlight of the first part of the game, his 43rd—or, more correctly, his after-the-43rd—was the highlight of the playoff. For after making his 43rd move Fischer walked off the stage and stayed away for 35 minutes, protesting that the television crew working from an aperture at the side of the stage distracted him. His clock kept ticking away while he was off the stage.

Officials of the Icelandic Chess Federation and members of the Fischer delegation rushed backstage, and pressure was brought on the cameraman to leave. The camera, it was reported, was dismantled. Fischer returned and, on his 56th move, resigned. Once more he had failed to get the better of Spassky.

Schmid, the referee, said that he had had no part in the decision to eject the cameraman and that problems about filming were not in his jurisdiction. He warned Fischer that if he persisted in his objections there would be trouble. He cited specifically two rules in the contract governing the match.

Rule 17 involved the sportsmanship of the players, and specified that it was forbidden to disturb an opponent on the move. In his opinion, Schmid said, the protest and walkout had disturbed Spassky.

Rule 21 stated that television coverage, as part of the agreement among the parties to the match, was to be permitted.

Fischer, according to Schmid, claimed that since he personally had not signed any agreement the rules did not apply to him. But Schmid—who was trained as a lawyer—said that since Fischer had started the match without making an objection, he legally was considered to have agreed to the rules.

A spokesman for Fischer said that the temperamental American objected not only to the television equipment, but also to the popping of flash bulbs in the audience. He would, the spokesman said, boycott the following day's game unless all cameras—private ones in the audience as well as TV cameras—were forbidden in the auditorium.

The next day, when he was scheduled to play White, and possibly break through the magic circle that many were willing to believe Spassky had drawn around him—he had never, up to that point, been able to defeat Spassky—Fischer did indeed boycott the game. He stayed locked in his hotel room.

At 5 P.M. precisely Spassky appeared on the stage of Exhibition Hall. Since he had the black pieces, he did not have the move. Schmid, in accordance with the rules, started Fischer's clock.

Spassky sat before the chessboard, looking uncomfortable, for about five minutes, then got up and left the stage. The audience of about 1,000 sat glued in their seats, watching the two empty chairs, for about an hour, with a sort of mesmerized fascination. Though there were no players, the audience remained dead silent.

Fischer's clock kept ticking away. A projection of it was shown on the closed-circuit television screen, and the audience could literally see the minutes slipping by.

While the clock ticked and the audience sat staring at the non-game going on—or not going on—on the stage, frantic efforts were being made to get the match going again. The Icelandic grandmaster Fridrik Olafsson, a friend of Fischer's and one of the most respected figures in the chess world, rushed to Fischer's room. Outside, a police car stood by, its motor running. And inside the hotel room, Lombardy was urging Fischer to play.

Under Rule 5 of the match, a player had one hour from the time his clock was started to begin play. If he failed to show up, the game was to be declared forfeit.

At 5:30 P.M., with half of Fischer's hour gone, his lawyer Davis telephoned from New York and spoke with Richard C. Stein, the attorney for Chester Fox, Inc., the company that had the contract with the Icelandic Chess Federation for exclusive film and television coverage. Davis proposed that, for that game only—the second—the TV cameras be removed, pending further discussion. Stein agreed. He called Lombardy on a hot line that had been set up from Fischer's room to Exhibition Hall.

But the point at issue, with Fox willing to forgo the cameras, had switched. It was now the elapsed time on Fischer's clock. Fischer demanded that it be turned back. Schmid said it couldn't be done. The rules had been bent almost out of shape several times already. "There has to be some limit," the referee said.

Fischer refused to budge.

When Fischer's clock reached the hour mark, Schmid walked to the front of the stage and announced that, under Rule 5, Spassky was the winner of the second game by a forfeit. The Russian appeared on stage, murmured, "It is a great pity," to Schmid, and was given a standing ovation by the crowd.

Fischer, who was reported to be in a state of wild agitation, refused to comment after the forfeit. Lombardy, still at the hotel, would say only: "We are hoping against hope that something can be worked out."

Fischer had until midnight—it was then 6 P.M.—to file a formal protest, and the referee was notified that there would be one.

The Russians were not commenting, either, but many chess enthusiasts were. Icelanders filing out of Exhibition Hall were making such comments as: "He has gone out of his mind," or "He is afraid to meet Spassky." Americans were volubly deploring Fischer's "disgraceful" behavior and some were heard apologizing to Icelanders in the name of America. Resentment and anger were expressed by the many visitors who had planned vacations around the match.

And mingled with all the anger and resentment was a curious undercurrent of sadness that so great and indeed, so creative, a chess mind should have acted in such a fashion.

There were also many references to the fact that Fischer, who had at first objected to the choice of Iceland because it did not have adequate television facilities, should now be walking out on the match because of a television hook-up.

"It's just an excuse," one Icelander said—and many seemed to agree—"the real reason is that he's afraid to play Spassky."

The supporting actors in the drama had not been idle in the hours before Schmid declared that Fischer had forfeited the second game.

After Fischer's protest and 35-minute walkout the previous day, Stein had arranged to discuss the matter. He, Lombardy and Cramer stayed up most of the night trying to work something out. They talked in one room and relayed the gist of their conversations to Fischer by telephone, who never appeared for the talks.

It had been suggested at that all-night meeting that Stein write a letter to Fischer, and he did so. The draft, dated July 13 and addressed to "Mr. Robert J. Fischer, challenger for the Chess Championship of the World," said:

"Dear Bobby:

"I am taking the liberty of addressing this

note to you personally, in the sincere hope that you will reconsider your position to discontinue filming the match.

"My appeal is based on two points which I ask you to consider.

"One. The ultimate purpose is to produce a first-quality product for the televising of these games throughout the world. With this end in mind, we urgently want to accommodate you in any practical way as to placement of equipment so as not to interfere with your concentration, while meeting the technical requirements for good filming.

"Two. Further, as an American, I can only express my admiration and appreciation for the elevation of chess in the eyes of the people of the States, through your Herculean efforts. Therefore, I emphasize the absolute need for using television for furthering your aims in that direction. As a folk hero of the Americans, you must permit millions of Americans to share this experience with you in their homes, for the benefit of chess and for the benefit of the rest of the world.

"I have been asked to discuss any thoughts that you might have on this problem, which distresses us all and which we are eager and anxious to ameliorate. In this way surely we can come to a reasonable agreement."

Stein explained to the American delegation that neither Fox nor the Icelandic Chess Federation would back down on TV and film coverage. Fox, he said, had made a "substantial investment" and the federation was counting on TV and film proceeds to help offset the deficit it had run up. "Their entire financial structure depends on it," he said.

No agreement had been reached by the morning of the day on which the second game was to be played and, in an effort to please Fischer, technicians placed the film and TV cameras in tunnels adjacent to the stage. A four-inch hole was bored for each lens. Only one operator was to be at a camera, and the operator was not to wear shoes or carry coins or anything else that might rattle or make noise.

The installations were tested in the afternoon. They were invisible from the players' table and, while in operation, could not be heard.

But Fischer refused to visit the hall to see or hear for himself. The mere knowledge that the cameras were present was enough to unsettle him, he said, and he wanted them off the premises.

Stein described Fischer's behavior as inconsiderate and selfish.

"I for one," he said, "have an obligation to stand up. You cannot permit anyone to run roughshod over other people."

But Fischer remained adamant, refused to play and wound up forfeiting the game and falling behind in the overall score. After the declaration of forfeit by Schmid the score of the match stood officially at 2–0 in Spassky's favor.

According to the rules, Schmid said, the remaining games had to be started. The charade would continue in three days—it was then Thursday and the next game was scheduled for Sunday. If Fischer left the country there would be an excuse for declaring the match over. Or the central committee of FIDE could convene for a special ruling to end the match. But unless either of those things happened, the match—or non-match—would have to go on.

"My stomach is churning," said Schmid, who was looking considerably less dapper than he had up to then.

Fischer filed his appeal, getting it in just under the midnight deadline. He appeared, however, to have made an error in a crucial paragraph. Recounting the events that led up to his decision, Fischer wrote:

"When I asked my representative to report the conditions at the playing hall for today's game [the second game] I learned at 1 P.M. and was told again at 4 P.M. that all three [camera] shooting sites which had been removed for the adjourned game at my insistence were in full operation, focused on the playing table, and had been returned to the positions they occupied on the opening day."

In fact, the television towers had been taken out of the hall for the adjourned game and the cameras had been moved to positions where they were invisible and inaudible.

Fischer went on to say in his letter of protest to Schmid that playing conditions were "grossly below the minimum standards" and that the organizers of the match were more eager to placate the "movie-camera gang than to provide playing conditions worthy of the world's chess championship."

Schmid's decision to grant the forfeit was taken up by a four-man committee consisting of Cramer, Krogius and two Icelanders, Gudmundur Arnlaugsson, the assistant referee, and Baldur Möller, a member of the Icelandic Chess Federation.

Before the committee met, Fischer was represented by Davis, who had arrived from New York a few hours earlier. Geller stated the Russian position. The committee heard their arguments and retired to consider the situation.

The panel upheld Schmid, saying the referee had had no choice. His decision, they said, was final. The forfeit would stand. As for Fischer's protests about noise, the committee said it could say nothing about so personal a matter. It invited the two players and their representatives to inspect the hall once more.

That night, Davis said the situation was "still up in the air" and could "come to a head in 48 hours." In any event, nothing would be decided within the next 24 hours because Fischer had begun his observance of the Sabbath and, following his custom, had cut himself off from the rest of the world.

The forfeit, the non-games and the still up-in-the-air situation created a sticky mess all around. What about the tickets that had been sold in advance? Would they have to be taken back? Would the non-game charade have to take place enough times to give Spassky a score of 12 points on forfeits?

Would the champion have to show up at each non-game to qualify? And what about the purse? Would it be split as originally planned—five-eighths to the winner, three-eighths to the loser—after the non-match was over? Or would Spassky be entitled to the entire prize? How about the other rights involved?

At that point the world championship match looked far more like a legal encounter than a chess contest. It was, it seemed, going to be fought out not on the stage of Exhibition Hall, but in courtrooms, possibly in New York, possibly in Iceland, possibly in Amsterdam, perhaps in Moscow. And perhaps in all of those places.

In Amsterdam Dr. Euwe expressed the opinion that Schmid was still the proper arbiter, but he conceded that "if this situation continues" FIDE would have to "consider whether to step in." Dr. Euwe, who had dealt with Fischer's protests and demands, with postponements, with haggling, with Russian anger, said: "The limit has been reached, and is even transgressed."

On Saturday, July 15, further attempts were made to bring the match back to life. A cablegram campaign was begun, a series of meetings was held and the decibel content of Exhibition Hall was measured again.

Cramer said that Fischer was adamant. Chester Fox, said Cramer, had "deceived" Fischer by installing noisy television equipment. But beyond that, and apparently more important, was the forfeiture ruling. Unless that was wiped off the books, he said, Fischer would not play.

In an effort to break the impasse, Marshall suggested that the appeals committee delay signing the forfeiture ruling. It would then, he said, be a pro-tem ruling that could be so considered later. With the forfeited game held in abeyance, the next game could be played, with Fischer having the white pieces.

A meeting was planned to discuss this proposal, though it seemed unlikely that the Soviet delegation would be willing to go along with it. That delegation, in fact, which had not been making waves, was now considering some protests of its own. Spassky—the calm, reasonable Spassky—was said to be annoyed by all the delays and postponements and protests. (The war of nerves, said the holders of the psychological-warfare theory, was working; Spassky was losing his cool.)

The cablegram campaign was begun by Americans in Reykjavik. They telephoned friends at home, urging them to send off cables to Fischer, and Fischer was said to have received large numbers of such communications.

One American at home did more than cable. He telephoned Fischer, asking him please to go on with the match for the sake not only of chess, but of his country as well. Fischer, who doesn't often talk to callers, accepted that call. It was from Henry Kissinger, President Nixon's man-about-the-world and chief foreign-affairs adviser.

The inspection of Exhibition Hall was made by the head of the Reykjavik Institute of Public Health. Reporting to the Icelandic Chess Federation, he said he had found the sound level in Exhibition Hall to be about 55 decibels with the cameras off and exactly the same—55 decibels—with them in operation.

As Sunday, July 16, approached, the status of the match was as clouded as it had ever been. More so, perhaps, because Fischer had made reservations on all three flights scheduled to leave Reykjavik that day.

As the day dawned, nobody would have given much of a chance for the game to take place. The meetings that had been held the previous day and night and that had continued through the early-morning hours had produced only an affirmation of the forfeit. Cramer, who had abstained in the committee vote, walked out of the deliberations, charging that Krogius was trying to sabotage the match.

What saved the day, the game and the match was a decision by Schmid to move the site of the playing from the main hall to a small room ordinarily used for table tennis. The only non-chess equipment in the room was a closed-circuit television camera—something Fischer had never protested about.

"I made the decision just to save the match," Schmid said.

Film and broadcast television were out, but Stein, the lawyer for Chester Fox, said he would do nothing to disrupt the game. And, he added, "we won't do anything to disrupt Tuesday's game" either.

"We are not the least bit interested in creating any friction to disrupt the games," he said in New York, but he added that he could not "just stand idly by and let such a substantial investment be destroyed."

Stein said that Fischer "knew everything in advance . . . certainly he was aware that TV cameras were to be operating." And he recalled that Fischer's original objection to Reykjavik had been that it had no TV facilities.

"Everything," said Stein, "is subject to negotiation."

Fischer canceled his flight reservations out of Reykjavik and showed up in the little table-tennis room after having sent Lombardy and Marshall to inspect the new site. They assured him there was absolute privacy there—and no film or broadcast-television cameras.

The match once more moved into the on-again status.

Spassky, as usual, showed up on time. Fischer walked in 10 minutes later—to surprised laughter and a smattering of applause from the audience of about 1,000 who had paid their $5 each to watch the action on a screen. The players shook hands and Spassky removed his jacket and hung it on the back of his chair.

As before, they were studies in immobility during the play, both leaning forward across the board, not eyeball to eyeball, but rather forehead to forehead. They looked not at each other, but at the board, concentrating fiercely on the position. From time to time one would rise and stretch his legs.

The game, like the first, went for 41 moves, with Fischer sealing his reply at the end and handing the envelope to Schmid. In the opinion of many experts, Fischer had a won game. He was ahead by a pawn and had strong mating threats.

"At least a draw and probably a win," said Olafsson.

"It is a clear win for Fischer," said the Yugoslav grandmaster Dragoljub Janosevic.

From the beginning it had been clear that Fischer was going to make a strong effort to seize the initiative from Spassky. He had to. He went into the game on the short side of a 2–0 score and the road ahead was obviously going to be a rough one.

Shortly after the adjournment the Russians delivered a protest to Schmid demanding that the playoff the following day, as well as all future games, be played on the stage of Exhibition Hall. Meetings to thrash out the issue were scheduled for the following day, raising the possibility that the action would shift again from the chessboard to the negotiating table.

Another protest was lodged, too—this one from the camera crews who had been prevented from working by Fischer. The American, they said in a letter to Schmid, had insulted them in his letter of protest, referring to them as "bungling unknowns who claim to be professional cameramen." If Fischer does not apologize, they said, they will sue him for libel.

And thus, though the match had been resurrected, the by-now normal air of uncertainty was still hanging heavily over it.

The following day—Monday, July 17—Fischer won, without even being there. It was his first victory over Spassky, not only in the match, but in the entire record of their confrontations over the board.

Spassky showed up promptly at 5 in Exhibition Hall. He had notified Schmid, in a personal letter rather than a formal protest, the previous night, that the upstairs table-tennis room was unsatisfactory. There was too much noise from traffic outside, children could be heard playing in the streets and the air-conditioner made a racket.

Fischer agreed to play in the main room, provided that no filming took place. Could his amenableness, some people asked, have stemmed from his realization that he had a winning game and was about to break the "hex" Spassky had long seemed to have imposed?

The cameras were banned. Gudmundur Thorarinsson, president of the Icelandic Chess Federation, said the decision had been a difficult one that imposed considerable financial hardship on the match sponsors.

"But this is a chess match," he said. "The filming is not the first priority. The chess match is the first priority. If this is the only way the match can go on, then we must take it."

Fischer showed up, as usual, late. About 15 minutes late. "What happened?" he asked, rushing breathlessly onto the stage. Schmid told him. Schmid had opened Fischer's sealed move, read it, and moved the piece on the board—41 . . . B-Q6ch. There was something forlorn about Spassky, alone on the stage, as Schmid opened the envelope and made the move. The champion looked at the board and at his hopelessly lost position, and he resigned.

Schmid walked to the front of the stage and said to the small audience: "I am sorry. The game is over. Mr. Spassky resigns."

The third game was over. The score stood at 2–1 in Spassky's favor. Fischer had, at last, defeated Spassky, and he had done it with the black pieces. He seemed to be in good spirits.

For the first time since the negotiations for the match had begun back in January, there seemed to be no immediate threat that it would not continue. Fischer had scored. The forfeit—Davis had said he would sue if it was not removed (and he didn't) and Fischer had said he would boycott the games if it wasn't (and he didn't)—was still on the books. But for the moment, at any rate, it was in the background. It could be taken up by FIDE in the fall, if neceessary.

But perhaps Fischer felt that it would not be necessary. Perhaps he felt that, no longer playing under the Indian sign Spassky had put on him, he would not even need that point. And so he played.

With the third game, the principal battlefield for the world championship of chess shifted to where the world had expected it to be—the chessboard. The major weapons in the battle became, not protests and counter-protests, demands and counter-demands, but rooks and queens, chessmen and chess squares. Minor clashes still took place from time to time away from the main arena, but the real action—the hand-to-hand (or head-to-head) combat—took place on the stage of Laugardalshöll, the exhibition hall, as champion and challenger fought for the crown.

One of the skirmishes that kept breaking out on the sidelines was the film and television issue. Chester Fox, who held the exclusive contract with the Icelandic Chess Federation for all film rights, including television film, tried to get footage without making the main subject of his footage—Fischer—walk out and upset everyone's apple cart, not just Chester Fox's.

The start of the fourth game, for example, was delayed while Fischer searched the second floor of the hall making sure that the film and TV cameras had been removed. The cameras had been there 20 minutes before game time.

"I put the cameras in every day," Fox said. "That's what my contract reads. And they are ordered out every day, because Fischer threatens to leave."

Fox's lawyer, Richard C. Stein, met several times with Fischer's lawyers and others in attempts to work out an agreement acceptable to all.

When reports began circulating during the third week in July that Fox was out and that an American Broadcasting Corporation unit was taking over, Fox said angrily: "I am not out of it." As for arrangements made in New York by Stein and Fischer's lawyer Marshall, Fox said: "I signed nothing and I own the corporation, no matter what deal is made between Stein, Marshall and the American Broadcasting Corporation."

Nevertheless, on July 27, when the eighth game of the match was filmed (it was the first game to be filmed since the opener), Fox issued a statement saying: "An agreement has been reached between all parties which will permit filming to continue. Chester Fox and Company, Inc., has contracted A. B. C. to supervise filming in the playing hall."

The new producer, Lorne Hassan, was allowed to place one camera in the projection booth on the main floor and two more on the sides of the hall at the balcony rail. The two cameramen sat on the floor, where they were not visible from the stage, and one of them rested his camera on a corrugated carton with the lens just clearing the balcony edge.

Even with these precautions Fischer was suspicious. When he walked on stage he looked around, then had a few words with the referee. He heard noise, he said. Schmid went to the projection booth and then assured Fischer the camera was inaudible.

The following day, A. B. C. announced it was withdrawing its camera crews from Iceland and giving up its attempts to film the match. The announcement followed a statement by Fischer that he would not participate in the next game unless the cameras were removed. He was said to have been furious when he learned that the eighth game had been filmed; he complained that no one had told him about the filming.

Although a representative of the Icelandic Chess Federation said it had been informed by Marshall that Fischer had given his approval for the filming, A. B. C. said it was willing to accept Fischer's statement that he had never been informed. "We are sorry that you were unaware of their placement," Roone Arledge, president of A. B. C. Sports, said of the cameras in a telegram to Fischer.

On August 4, the Icelandic Chess Federation released the camera crew, which had, despite the all but hopeless outlook, been standing by. The Federation had counted on revenue from films and TV to help meet the deficit for sponsoring the match.

"It's hard, it's hard," said Thorarinsson, the Federation's president.

Fox, however, remained in Reykjavik, trying to recoup what he could through the sale of still pictures. And from time to time he threatened to sue.

On August 15, when the score and the dwindling number of games remaining made Fischer's ultimate victory all but an absolute certainty, Fox said he planned to sue Fischer "for every cent we can lay hands on."

"No figures have been worked out yet," he said, "but $1-million makes sense" for the loss of the television-film revenue.

But television, as Thorarinsson had said, was of only secondary interest. With or without a TV screen the world was watching Fischer and Spassky, their attacks, their defenses, their thrusts and parries. And their surprises.

For surprise played, or seemed to play, a major role, to be a major weapon, in the battle.

Fischer, for example, who throughout his career had almost invariably opened with 1 P-K4, unexpectedly opened with 1 P-QB4 in the sixth game. It must have been totally unexpected; the Russians had undoubtedly analyzed and reanalyzed every one of Fischer's games. All but three of them had begun with 1 P-K4.

In the previous game—the fifth—Fischer had pounced on an error by Spassky and, though playing the ordinarily defensive black pieces, had forced the champion to resign. That had brought the score in the match to 2½–2½, despite the point lost by Fischer in the forfeited second game.

Now Fischer drew ahead by a full point. The surprise opening, plus the loss of the game, must have been a powerful psychological blow to Spassky. And, on the same day—it was July 20—Fischer's "14 points" were leaked (or stolen). Though the American delegation said it was much ado about nothing, and Cramer said it was only a "punch list" of points that remained to be cleared, it caused something of a stir in what had become the chess capital of the world.

The list contained such items as a request for a private swimming pool, a new automobile, a wider choice of restaurants in which to dine, an indoor tennis court, pocket money to be paid in advance and a broader selection of current reading material.

Public opinion was divided. During the initial maneuvers and skirmishes, when it often seemed that there would be no match at all, sympathies were heavily with Spassky and feelings ran high against Fischer. The new list of demands led at least one Icelandic chess enthusiast to say what others had perhaps hinted at: that Spassky could have walked out on Fischer half a dozen times, taking the title with him, and that "no one in Iceland would have blamed him."

But there were those who were willing to forgive Fischer everything, because of the brilliance of his chess-playing. It was not that Fischer could do no wrong; rather it was that none of the wrongs mattered. Only the chess games themselves counted.

After the sixth game a number of grandmasters said Spassky seemed to have become a changed man, playing especially badly. But the same thing had been said before, about Taimanov, about Larsen, about Petrosian.

Changed or not, Spassky was, at that point, far from ready to lie down and let Fischer roll over him. In the next game he used his own surprise, opening with Fischer's own favorite 1 P-K4. He arrived, as he normally did, precisely at 5 P.M. And Fischer arrived on what, for him, was on schedule—about 15 minutes late. (Here, too, the war of nerves was apparently still going on. It continued throughout the match, with sometimes one player arriving late, sometimes the other. If a player walked on stage and found his opponent's chair empty, he would, as often as not, walk off again, then appear later, after the second player had shown up. In the latter part of the match the entrances and exits took on something of the appearance of a complex pavanne.) The seventh game ended in a draw.

In the eighth game, in which Fischer toyed with Spassky before crushing him and moving into a commanding 5–3 lead in match points, the champion looked weary. While Fischer leaned back, gently moving to and fro in his swivel chair, Spassky gazed on his shattered position and passed his hand through his hair—a gesture of despair that was to be seen again and again.

By the end of July the conversation among the gaggle of grandmasters gathered in Reykjavik was full of speculation about Spassky's breakdown. He had arrived in Iceland in high spirits, looking relaxed, proud and healthy. He was, after all, the world champion. He had conquered the world's leading players (including Fischer, who had not yet been able to beat him).

Now he had been humbled and discomfited, to the point where he was making blunders that even novices manage to avoid. He had, it seemed, fallen victim to "Fischer fear."

On July 30, Spassky asked for and was granted a postponement, on medical grounds, of the scheduled ninth game. He had, at that time, been able to gain only 1 point in the previous six games, and he trailed 5 to 3.

In the eighth game he had taken about an hour on one move, made two elementary blunders and, in general, had played listlessly.

"Spassky is not Spassky," the Argentine grandmaster Miguel Najdorf said on the morning of the 30th. "I know him well, and he is strange. He does not smile. He acts like a man in jail. There is something on his mind besides Fischer."

Normally, said Najdorf, Spassky is gregarious and enjoys having a bit of fun. In Reykjavik he was acting like a man on the way to the gallows. He was surrounded by Soviet aides and was never seen on his own.

"If the Russians would leave him alone," Najdorf suggested, "he would play much better chess."

Spassky, of course, was carrying a burden that Fischer was not laden with: he was playing not only for himself, but also for the Soviet government, the Soviet system. He represented an ideology. Soviet chess players were supreme, so the theory went, because the Soviet social, political and governmental system was so much better. Fischer—though he may have accused the Russians of chess collusion—had no political load on his shoulders.

In the ninth game (which was drawn) Spassky played cleanly and without error, but he looked restless and nervous. He walked off the stage a great deal and had a haggard look about him. It may have been the residual effects of the cold that led him to seek the postponement of the game; it may have been "Fischer fever"; it may have been a little of each.

Grandmaster Larsen, who had arrived in Reykjavik the day before the ninth game, said that Spassky was not playing aggressively because he obviously wanted to settle his nerves.

"Nerves," Larsen said, "are everything. It is not the chess game that wins the match. It is nerves."

Later, Larsen said that Fischer, too, was nervous, "but at the board he changes immediately."

"He controls himself," Larsen said. "I mean complete control. This is something very remarkable."

Still, Larsen refused to count Spassky out.

The 10th game, in which Spassky resigned on the

56th move, put Fischer ahead 6½ to 3½, and few people—perhaps Larsen was all but alone—gave Spassky much chance of retaining the title.

"There is very little hope for Spassky," said Svetozar Gligoric, the Yugoslav grandmaster.

Nevertheless, in the 11th game, Spassky fought back, trapping a queen that Fischer had audaciously sent into the champion's territory, winning the game and cutting Fischer's lead to 2 points. The score became 6½–4½. Had Spassky lost the game, Fischer's substantial lead would have become virtually insurmountable. Even a draw would have been bad for Spassky at that point, because of the psychologically crushing effect it would have had. He was playing White—the side with the initiative, the aggressive, fighting side—and he had to win, for he had defeated Fischer only once thus far, in the first game.

"It was Spassky's best game to date," said Lubomir Kavalek, the Czech grandmaster who had moved to the United States. "It was deep and profound."

Spassky held the initiative from beginning to end, steering the action into more complicated, denser play than the sort that is Fischer's specialty.

Earlier that day the champion was reported to have said that he was not enjoying the match much. After the game he said "the rest of the match will be more interesting for me."

Spassky apparently no longer intended to play a waiting or cautious game; he meant to slug it out.

During the 12th game, Fischer offered a draw by repetition of moves. Spassky refused it by playing a move that made the repetition impossible. The game, however, drifted into a position where neither side had a chance of winning, and a draw was agreed upon at the 56th move. It could have been offered and accepted earlier, but grandmasters do not like to offer draws unless they are sure their opponents will accept.

There is a psychology of the draw. Often, a player who has offered a draw, and then is turned down, feels humiliated, and starts to play rashly to teach his opponent a lesson. This is suicidal, and the "I'll show him" attitude has led to ghastly losses that never should have happened.

In the 12th game, then, Spassky waited until there could be no doubt about the draw. During the game, some grandmasters discussed the reason for Fischer's apparent determination to play out a game that had no possibility of victory. One obvious answer was that Fischer hates a draw, and plays to win. Another, however, was that he might have been trying to wear Spassky down. He is six years younger than the champion, and the harder he made Spassky work, the more fatigued—and thus error-prone—the champion would become.

After the 12th game, Fischer fired off a letter to Schmid, the referee, complaining about noise and playing conditions. It said: "Sir: I most vigorously protest the excessive spectator noise in the hall today, and your failure to take proper action about it when I complained about it to you, and the failure of the organizers to heed several earlier complaints of improper playing conditions and closeness of spectators.

"The exhibition hall was not designed for a chess match, and it has very little acoustical treatment of the type required for such an event. Hence special precautions are most necessary, one of which is the removal of at least seven of the rows of seats closest to the stage. The spectators are so close, and so noisy, and the acoustics are so poor, that I can hear them opening candy wrappers and I hear bits of conversation, as well as coughing, laughing, and so on.

"This is not suitable for a world championship match, and I demand that you and the organizers take immediate action to insure full and complete correction of these disgraceful conditions and furnish me a full report of what is to be done."

It was signed, "Yours truly, Bobby Fischer."

Thorarinsson, the chess federation president, said that efforts would be made to reduce noise but that no seats would be removed. Schmid said the letter was "just a normal letter by Bobby's standards."

The 13th game was played with all seats intact. It was a long game—going 74 moves—and in a sense it was a heartbreaker for Spassky, who was outstayed and outplayed. It put Fischer within 4½ points of the title and, when it was over, the prevalent feeling was that, for all practical purposes, the match was already finished. Spassky, it was felt, could not possibly overcome a three-point handicap so late in the match.

At that stage, Spassky could no longer afford to play for the half points he would get from draws; he would have to play to win, and he would need to win three games just to pull up even with Fischer. Many grandmasters felt that the loss of that 13th game might well have broken Spassky's spirit.

The champion had come to the adjourned position, after 42 moves with good drawing chances. Lengthy analysis overnight had convinced him and Geller that, even though he was a pawn down, he could hold Fischer to a draw. With the resumption of the game, Spassky defended brilliantly. He immobilized Fischer's rook, but then Fischer—in a move that electrified the experts—sacrificed a pawn to get his king, and, eventually, his rook, into action. The ending was one of Fischer's most brilliant performances, and there were a few cheers from the audience.

Toward the end, when the game slipped from his control, the champion's normally impassive face took on a sick look, and his movements became slow. Fischer, who had also looked drawn, began to show confidence, lolling back and sipping ice water or a cola drink. Veteran Fischer-watchers knew that at that point he had the game under control.

When it was over, Spassky appeared stunned. He stared at the board and then sat down to replay the last few moves with the referee, obviously searching for the spot at which he had gone wrong. Then, looking crushed, he slowly left the stage to a round of sympathetic applause.

There had been times when the playing hall was less than half filled and times when it was jammed. For that game—the 13th—it had been more than jammed. Those who ordinarily wandered around the building, talking, eating, drinking and following the game on the TV monitors, all seemed to crowd into the playing hall.

There was standing room only. And yet, despite

the size of the audience, the hall was quieter than it had ever been. The silence accentuated the tension; it made it almost tangible. Every eye was directed toward the stage or toward the huge electronic board above the stage.

The audience was almost as motionless as the two figures flanking the chess table on stage.

How, non-chess players sometimes ask, how can there be excitement in a game in which two people stare at a board or at each other for half an hour or more?

Anyone who had been in the playing hall that day would have known—would have felt—the answer. The excitement, the tension, held everyone there in its grip. It was as though 2,500 people at once were holding their breath, waiting. And when at last it was over, and Spassky had lost, the effect was like a huge sigh.

After that devastating blow Spassky once more sought a postponement. The official match physician, Ulfar Thordarson, was called to Spassky's hotel room, and he issued a certificate to Schmid that said:

"I undersigned have today at this time (1020 GMT) examined Boris Spassky, who does not feel well. I have on medical reasons advised him not to play the scheduled game today."

The game—like the first postponed game, scheduled for a Sunday—was put off to Tuesday.

Fischer, through Cramer, asked for a photocopy of the medical certificate, hinting that the Americans did not believe that Spassky was indeed ill. But the request drew nothing more than an expression of annoyance from Schmid, who called it improper.

"Spassky does not feel well," the referee said. "That is enough."

In the 14th game, played after the second postponement, Fischer blundered on his 19th move, and grandmasters in the hall wondered how long he would take to resign. But then, on his 27th turn, Spassky blundered in turn, letting victory slip through his fingers. Fischer capitalized on the blunder immediately, and Spassky, realizing what he had done, looked away from the board, his face a wrinkle of misery.

"Spassky is three points behind," Grandmaster Lubomir Kavalec said, "and that is conducive to mistakes. The pressure is working on him."

To add to Spassky's woes, his wife, for the first time, was in the audience and she, too, had seen him blunder away a victory. The game ended in a draw, making the score 8½–5½.

As soon as the game ended, Fischer fired off a telegram to Dr. Euwe in Amsterdam. The telegram, signed by Cramer, said that if playing conditions were not immediately improved, Fischer would "demand" that the remaining games be played in a private room. He renewed his demand for the removal of the first seven rows of seats, called for more ushers to enforce silence and called Schmid and the Icelandic Chess Federation "arrogant and inconsiderate."

An Icelandic chess official replied that no other championship match in history had had better playing conditions and that the match organizers would not even think of removing the first seven rows.

As for Dr. Euwe, he said the dispute was not within his province.

The 15th game was played with all seats intact and with the audience apparently sensitively conscious of the battle over noise. Many people actually tip-toed into the playing hall. Still, Fischer continued to bombard chess officials with letters of complaint and threats to quit. Cramer demanded that Schmid "do something better than wave your hand from time to time."

"What do they expect him to do," one observer asked. "Use nerve gas?"

In the game itself, Fischer once more miscalculated in the early part, allowing Spassky to win a pawn. But then, as before, Spassky erred. "First Spassky should have won," said a grandmaster, "and then Fischer should have won."

Neither did, and the game ended in a draw after 43 moves, making the score 9 to 6.

Before the start of the 16th game, Fischer made an attempt to have the playing site shifted to a private room. Schmid turned him down, saying the game would be played on the stage unless there was a disturbance in the auditorium. Several times during the game Fischer complained to the referee about noise, but he did not press his complaints, and the site was not changed.

During the day the Icelandic Chess Federation denied that it was a party to Fox's suit against Fischer, which had been filed for $1.75 million. It would be, said Thorarinsson, the federation's president, "a ghastly mistake if we are named as co-plaintiff."

"There have been enough problems so far," Thorarinsson said.

Though Spassky played well, Fischer parried all the threats and, after 60 moves, both sides agreed to another draw. The score became 9½–6½.

In the next game, the 17th, Spassky—rapidly being backed into a corner from which no escape would be possible—made a powerful bid for victory, sacrificing a pawn early in the game for attacking chances. He seemed to be throwing everything he had at his challenger, playing aggressively, dynamically. Still, Fischer met his every thrust skillfully. At adjournment, after 41 moves, Spassky had a slight edge, but it proved to be short of enough. The resumed game ended, after only five moves, in a draw. The score became 10 to 7, leaving only 2½ points between Fischer and the title.

It was during the 17th game that the Russians charged that the Americans might be using "electronic devices and a chemical substance" to weaken Spassky's playing ability. In a long written statement, Geller demanded that Schmid and the match sponsors examine the playing hall "with the assistance of competent experts" to determine whether the Americans were using non-chess means to influence Spassky.

"It is surprising that the Americans can be found in the playing hall when the games are not taking place, even at night," Geller wrote. And, speaking of Spassky's performance, he said:

"Having known [Spassky] for so many years, it is the first time that I observe such unusual slackening of concentration and display of impulsiveness in his playing which I cannot account for by [Fischer's] exclusively impressive playing."

Geller mentioned Fischer's special chair and the special lighting installed at Fischer's insistence, and hinted that Fischer was using psychological means of "unbalancing Mr. B. Spassky and making him lose his fighting spirit."

Why, Geller asked, was Fischer so adamantly opposed to having the match filmed. Then, answering his own question, he said: "One of the reasons might be that he is anxious to get rid of the constant objective control over the behavior and physical state of the participants.

"All this may seem fantastic," Geller went on, "but some objective factors in this connection make us think of such seemingly fantastic suppositions."

Many non-participants thought the charges hilarious, and one suggested that the Icelandic Chess Federation "get James Bond 007 to investigate the hall."

But Schmid didn't laugh; it was his job to resolve the dispute somehow. Besides, he said, there had been some "fantastic things" from the American side, so why not from the Russian.

On August 24 two Icelandic experts investigated the lighting and the chairs. Dadi Augustin, an electronics engineer, discovered two dead flies in the lighting equipment and concluded there had been no tampering with the lights.

He also x-rayed the players' chairs and reported that they were identical in all respects and that neither contained anything unsual. (Geller had wondered why Fischer always insisted on using his own special chair.)

Sigmundur Gudbjarnason, a professor of chemistry, subjected scrapings from both chairs to chemical analysis and gas chromatography and concluded that there were no alien or toxic chemicals present in the body residues of either player.

The seating also produced some minor fireworks. Fischer's demand for the removal of the first seven rows had been rejected, but the organizers had agreed to remove two rows as a compromise. The Russians objected, and Geller sent a letter to Schmid saying:

"I am protesting against the change of the agreement of the match, to leave empty the first rows in the playing hall, which has been done without consent of the Soviet side. We request that the former situation in the playing hall be restored."

The protest was discussed by the American delegation, Schmid and the Icelandic Chess Federation. The Americans said that if the seats were restored there would be no more games. Schmid and Cramer exchanged angry words.

Finally it was decided to restore the seats but to rope off the first three rows and let no one sit in them.

In Moscow, there were reports, which were denied in Reykjavik, that the State Committee on Sports had recommended that Spassky return home in protest over Fischer's delays in appearing for the match and his flamboyant behavior. Spassky was also said to have been asked by Moscow whether, in the light of Fischer's behavior, the champion was in a frame of mind in which he could defeat the challenger.

Some sources in Iceland interpreted that as seeking to justify a demand for Fischer's disqualification, thus keeping the title—despite the outcome of the match in terms of points—in the Soviet Union.

The 18th game ended, like the four previous games, in a draw. Fischer, who had always had a reputation for playing all-out and declining draws, was apparently adopting a new attitude and was sliding into the world championship on half points.

On the day of the fifth consecutive draw—which made the score 10½–7½—Stein, Chester Fox's lawyer, said legal proceedings had been started to have Fischer's prize money attached. The following day a writ was served on Cramer, and Stein said he was leaving for England to attach Fischer's share of the $125,000 offered by Slater, the millionaire whose generosity had broken the pre-match hold-off.

The Icelandic Chess Federation, however, announced that it was waiving all shares in any suit against Fischer in return for promises from Fox to take no action against Fischer in Iceland.

With, at most, only six games remaining, Spassky seemed somehow to have revived, to have taken on new life, a new will to win. Speculation about this—as about almost everything else that had happened before and during the match—was wild. Was it the presence of his wife, Larisa? (Spassky, so unlike Fischer, enjoys and seems to benefit from the company of women.) Was it desperation? Or perhaps—quite the opposite—resignation and, therefore, a new relaxation that was letting him play up to his capabilities?

The 19th game was a case in point. Fireworks went off when Spassky, on his 18th move, gave up a knight in return for a king side attack and a phalanx of central pawns.

"Oh, oh," said one grandmaster, "hold onto your seat belts."

"Bobby's in a very tough position," said another.

And a third put his finger right on it. "What's gotten into Spassky?" he asked rhetorically. "This is the Spassky of old times."

And so it was. The Spassky whose chess had made him the champion of the world. The Spassky whose cool, precise and sometimes brilliant style had crushed the best there were—including Fischer.

But somehow, somewhere along the line in that 19th game, Spassky's powerful attack flagged, then fizzled. Fischer's 21 . . . Q-Q7 forced an exchange of queens and spelled finis to Spassky's assault. Many experts were puzzled.

"Such a strong attack," lamented Geller, "and nothing happened."

Gligoric offered the explanation, if such it could be called.

"That Bobby," he said, "he always escapes."

(If the experts were puzzled, many Icelanders weren't. They knew the answer: Spassky had somehow insulted or outraged the elves and, unless he managed to make amends, his case was hopeless. Elves are everywhere in Iceland, and many homes have an elves' rock, which is not to be moved. Whoever disturbs the elves or their homes will inevitably come down with boils, bad luck, fallen arches, constant headaches and, ultimately, disaster.

(When an airport was being built in the northern

city of Akureyri, the elves were disturbed by the construction work. The troubles never seemed to end. Drill bits broke, workmen broke their legs and arms, concrete cured before it was poured—everything was going wrong. Then the foreman made a deal with the chief elf: work was to stop for a year to give the elves time to find new homes. The elves agreed and, moreover, promised that there would never be an airplane accident at the airport.

(The government lived up to its part of the bargain, holding up work for a year. The elves did, too. There has never been an accident at Akureyri.

(The farm adjoining Exhibition Hall, Icelanders pointed out, is named Elves' Hill. Spassky, they think, must have crossed the elves. Or perhaps Fischer had made a deal with them. Perhaps, they said, if Spassky went out some night and spoke to the chief elf . . .

(But it would have to be done quickly, because the 19th game ended in a draw, making the score 8 to 11; Fischer needed only 1½ points—a victory and a draw or three draws—to become the new champion.)

The day after the 19th game, on August 28, Ivo Nei, who had arrived in Iceland with Spassky on June 21, said he was leaving. He was going home to Estonia, he said, to open his chess school. The end was in sight.

The 20th game was, in a sense, a replay of the 19th. Spassky, this time as Black, played hard, aggressive chess. Major pieces were exchanged early and a draw looked as though it was in the making. But Spassky continued to maneuver and, with slow, painstaking work, brought the game, at adjournment, to a position in which he had an edge. On the Black side, he had managed to wring what he could out of the game, bringing about an end game with winning possibilities.

But it was not to be. When the game resumed the next day, Spassky tried mightily to lure Fischer into erring. But the challenger refused to oblige, and Spassky was unable to convert his slight edge into a winning one. Another draw—the seventh in a row—was agreed upon, and Fischer stood only one point away from his goal.

And then came the 21st game.

PART TWO/The Games

Game One

The first game began with 1 P-Q4, a staid queen-pawn opening that eventually reverted to the Tarrasch Defense. Clearly, Spassky preferred a positional game. The Tarrasch—named for Siegbert Tarrasch, a grandmaster, theorist and writer who died in 1934—arises after 1 P-Q4, P-Q4; 2 P-QB4, P-K3; 3 N-QB3, P-QB4. It offers Black freedom for his pieces. Its drawback, and the element that has made it unpopular, is that in most cases Black must acquiesce in the isolation of his queen pawn.

Lately, however, the Tarrasch has been enjoying something of a comeback. The renewed interest has resulted from fresh examinations that have shown that White's task is anything but simple. Thus, even grandmasters like Tal and Keres have been experimenting with the Tarrasch.

This first game developed along general principles, with neither side showing any advantage. Everything was more or less standard. On his 11th move, PxP, White avoided the possibility of having to cope with an isolated center pawn, and Black pushed himself further along lines leading to a drawish end game. The exchange of material that followed— 11 . . . QxQ; 12 RxQ, BxP; 13 P-QN4, B-K2; 14 B-N2, B-Q2; 15 QR-B1, KR-Q1; 16 N/2-Q4, NxN; 17 NxN —left everything even, with prospects for a draw even greater than ever.

After another exchange following Black's 17 . . . B-R5, Black commanded the queen bishop file and White the queen file. White, however, invited even further simplification, which followed his 23 R-QB1, as well as his 27 N-B4. Two more moves and the position, if anything, was heading into what looked like an uneventful draw.

And then came Fischer's electrifying 29 . . . BxKRP.

Many chess analysts—most, in fact—saw this move as only one thing: an incredible blunder. Some put the symbol "??" after Fischer's move, indicating no doubt about the evaluation. But a more balanced analysis would make that symbol "?!" —indicating that the element of risk is high but that perhaps the move really is one with strong possibilities.

In any event, to label the move simply as a blunder is in itself a blunder. In reality, the move was based on fairly sound chess principles. The term "poisoned pawn" was also found in many appraisals and analyses, and perhaps it is a good description—certainly for a player of less than Fischer's caliber there would be a fatal dose of poison in a pawn left en prise that way by the world champion of chess.

But two pawns often defeat a bishop in an end game, and Fischer's seizing of the "poisoned" king rook pawn, after the exchanges that followed, left him with five pawns to Spassky's three. This would have meant obtaining winning chances if he had conducted the game properly and precisely.

BLACK/FISCHER

WHITE/SPASSKY

35 . . . K-Q3

Immediately after the loss of the bishop, Fischer pushed his king to Q3, centralizing it; it was in a far better spot than Spassky's king. But Spassky might have considered the idea too—the idea of a bishop vis-à-vis two pawns in the end game—and he must have been prepared for it.

Black kept his king centralized. His 37 . . . K-K5 made his king the dominant force in the center and attacked the only remaining white king-side pawn. White had to counter this thrust, and did so with 38 B-B5.

At adjournment, after Black's 40th move, Black still had drawing chances, and a slip by White at almost any point would have assured Black of a draw. A win seemed out of the question, for Black's king bishop pawn was obviously doomed and with its demise went, or would go, any chances for keeping Black's king-side pawns united and self-supporting.

When White's 41st move was unsealed at the resumption of the game the following day, it turned out to be the expected—indeed, the almost inevitable—PxP. Black recaptured with 41 . . . KxP and the Black pawn formation was split. But Black still had at his disposal means of keeping the White king from crossing over to the queen's side of the board, where the decisive action was going to take place.

White's 42 K-R5 was an attempt to get the king moving; it was correctly followed by Black's 42 . . . K-B4, preventing the white king from joining the battle.

What happened from that point on was, basically, a shifting of the action to the queen's side and a series of moves by White designed to keep his bishop on the most effective—actually, the vital—diagonal KN2–QR7. With 47 . . . K-B3, the white king became mobile and thereafter began crossing the board to the scene of the battle.

The black king knight pawn became a sacrifice (and a useless one) in an effort to keep the white king away from its goal. At the end, Black had no resources and virtually no moves at his disposal. Had the game gone on, the remaining white pawn would inevitably have been able to reach the eighth rank.

In one sense, the first game began with Black's 29th move. And it is still difficult to say whether Fischer's judgment was correct. He could have won. He certainly could have drawn. But he did neither. He lost.

What followed that 29th move was inaccurate play on Black's part that made the capture of the king rook pawn, in retrospect, look like a blunder. It was not. Fischer did, however, blunder away his chances in the play that followed, first missing a win and then a draw. His technique failed.

Thus Spassky gained the first point of the match not through any great combination, but through errors that Fischer made after the sacrifice of the bishop.

BLACK/FISCHER

WHITE/SPASSKY

Final Position

Following is the complete play-by-play score of the first game:

White Spassky	Black Fischer	White Spassky	Black Fischer
1 P-Q4	N-KB3	14 B-N2	B-Q2
2 P-QB4	P-K3	15 QR-B1	KR-Q1
3 N-KB3	P-Q4	16 N/2-Q4	NxN
4 N-B3	B-N5	17 NxN	B-R5
5 P-K3	O-O	18 B-N3	BxB
6 B-Q3	P-B4	19 NxB	RxRch
7 O-O	N-B3	20 RxR	R-QB1
8 P-QR3	B-R4	21 K-B1	K-B1
9 N-K2	QPxP	22 K-K2	N-K5
10 BxBP	B-N3	23 R-QB1	RxR
11 PxP	QxQ	24 BxR	P-B3
12 RxQ	BxP	25 N-R5	N-Q3
13 P-QN4	B-K2	26 K-Q3	B-Q1

White Spassky	Black Fischer	White Spassky	Black Fischer
27 N-B4	B-B2	42 K-R5	K-B4
28 NxN	BxN	43 B-K3	K-K5
29 P-N5	BxKRP	44 B-B2	K-B4
30 P-N3	P-KR4	45 B-R4	P-K4
31 K-K2	P-R5	46 B-N5	P-K5
32 K-B3	K-K2	47 B-K3	K-B3
33 K-N2	PxP	48 K-N4	K-K4
34 PxP	BxP	49 K-N5	K-Q4
35 KxB	K-Q3	50 K-B5	P-R4
36 P-R4	K-Q4	51 B-B2	P-N4
37 B-R3	K-K5	52 KxP	K-B5
38 B-B5	P-R3	53 K-B5	K-N5
39 P-N6	P-B4	54 KxP	KxP
40 K-R4	P-B5	55 K-Q5	K-N4
41 PxP	KxP	56 K-Q6	Resigns

SCORE: Spassky 1 Fischer 0

Game Two

Forfeit

SCORE: Spassky 2 Fischer 0

Game Three

In the third game, as in the first (the second game was the notorious non-game in which Spassky sat, alone and ill at ease, on the stage while Fischer, boycotting the game over the issue of television coverage, remained in his locked hotel room), Fischer played more sharply in the opening, stealing the initiative in the first few moves without being punished for it.

Spassky opened, as he did in the first (and, for him, successful) game, with a queen's pawn debut. Fischer steered this one into the lines of a Benoni, which gave him an immediate plus. After a few moves it became evident that Spassky had no counterpattern of his own.

White's 7 N-Q2 is somewhat more passive than the more frequently used 7 P-K4, and Black's immediate response to it, 7 . . . QN-Q2, indicated that he was prepared for—even inviting—a fight. This is certainly in line with Fischer's general approach to chess. He is not a draw-seeker, even when playing the Black side. He plays an all-out game.

If any further proof was needed of Fischer's approach, it came with his stunning 11th move, 11 . . . N-R4. Almost every grandmaster and expert at the scene felt the knight was misplaced at the side of the board. There is an old German saying that, translated into a weak rhyme in English, comes out as "a knight on the rim is dim." Despite the uninspired words, the thought is, in general, a correct one; a knight on the rim commands only half the squares he is capable of commanding, and he is far from the center; where he belongs.

Fischer, by playing the knight to KR4, invited Spassky to capture it.

The capture of the knight would, after the forced recapture by the king knight pawn, bring about a doubling of Fischer's king rook pawns and create a weakness

BLACK/FISCHER

WHITE/SPASSKY

11 . . . N-R4

in the king-side pawn structure. Fischer, however, no longer had to be concerned about the bishop operating on the light squares; it was gone, and Fischer was able to make use of the light squares.

The move 14 . . . Q-R5 posed direct threats to the white king and served another purpose that became evident in the following sequence. After 15 B-Q2, which continued Spassky's development, Fischer played the aggressive 15 . . . N-N5, with the obvious and immediate threat of mate at KR2, and Spassky was forced to counter this by exchanging knights— 16 NxN, PxN. This undoubled Black's king-side pawns and left him in a still aggressive position and with the bishop-pair.

Fischer might also have played 15 . . . N-B6ch, but after 16 PxN, B-K4, White could have moved his king rook over to create an escape hatch. Black would then have been playing a piece down and could not have carried through the attack.

On his 28th, 29th, 30th and 31st moves, White could do little more than shuttle one of his rooks back and forth between K2 and K3. If he had had more time, he might have been able to break out, but he was pressed—in good part because he had used half an hour studying Black's extraordinary 11th move.

After the exchanges that followed, White played 35 B-R6 but was then forced to retrench after 35 . . . Q-N3. Had he tried on his 35th move to capture Black's backward, blocked and isolated queen pawn, he could have been sharply rebuffed by 35 . . . QxP with the threat of . . . Q-Q8ch and . . . B-B3ch.

White's 37 K-B1 and 38 K-K2 were virtually forced. Black posed mating threats in profusion, and the king had to be moved out of his hemmed-in position. Nevertheless, a series of checks followed, and White, already in time trouble, was forced to find precise and accurate moves each time.

At adjournment, White was in critical difficulties. Few experts held out any hope for White, though some seemed to feel there was still some possibility of squeezing out a draw. Black did not take long to think about and seal his move.

When the game resumed, the sealed move turned

out to be the one that almost everyone expected—41 . . . B-Q6ch. There was no escape for White.

BLACK/FISCHER

WHITE/SPASSKY

Final Position

Following is the complete play of the third game:

White Spassky	Black Fischer	White Spassky	Black Fischer
1 P-Q4	N-KB3	22 QR-K1	Q-N3
2 P-QB4	P-K3	23 P-N3	R-K2
3 N-KB3	P-QB4	24 Q-Q3	R-N1
4 P-Q5	PxP	25 PxP	PxP
5 PxP	P-Q3	26 P-N4	P-B5
6 N-B3	P-KN3	27 Q-Q2	QR-K1
7 N-Q2	QN-Q2	28 R-K3	P-R4
8 P-K4	B-N2	29 R/3-K2	K-R2
9 B-K2	O-O	30 R-K3	K-N1
10 O-O	R-K1	31 R/3-K2	BxN
11 Q-B2	N-R4	32 QxB	RxP
12 BxN	PxB	33 RxR	RxR
13 N-B4	N-K4	34 RxR	QxR
14 N-K3	Q-R5	35 B-R6	Q-N3
15 B-Q2	N-N5	36 B-B1	Q-N8
16 NxN	PxN	37 K-B1	B-B4
17 B-B4	Q-B3	38 K-K2	Q-K5ch
18 P-KN3	B-Q2	39 Q-K3	Q-B7ch
19 P-QR4	P-N3	40 Q-Q2	Q-N6
20 KR-K1	P-QR3	41 Q-Q4	B-Q6ch
21 R-K2	P-N4	Resigns	

SCORE: Spassky 2 Fischer 1

Game Four

Fischer's victory in the third game was his first victory —ever—over Spassky. It must have had an exhilarating effect on him, especially since he defeated Spassky while playing the Black side, and the game must have depressed the champion. Nevertheless, in the fourth game Spassky made what amounted to a comeback. It might have been even more of a comeback—a victory instead of a draw—but Spassky fell victim to time, as he had before, and, with the clock hands putting pressure on him, he was unable to find the best line, the one that could and should have won for him.

The game began with the move everyone has come to expect from Fischer, 1 P-K4. It is his trademark. But the move that followed was as unexpected as the first was expected. Spassky played 1 . . . P-QB4, the Sicilian Defense. He is not known for this opening, this very popular Black line, because—though he is a powerful and precise player who can unleash devastating attacks —he is not the kind of player for whom the fighting Sicilian seems tailored.

It has been said that in many lines the Sicilian shows little relationship between the opening and the end game, because the tactical possibilities—almost a free-for-all—that crop up in the middle game minimize any direct links between the opening moves and the situation that emerges from the ensuing melee. Spassky, like Fischer, is a fabulous technician when it comes to end games, but plunging into a Sicilian reduces the possibility of seeing ahead to a favorable end game.

Add to this the fact that Fischer probably knows the Sicilian, in all its variations and sub-variations, as well as or better than any player alive, and it becomes a matter of great surprise for Spassky to reply with 1 . . . P-QB4.

Fischer chose to castle short, instead of long, meaning that the game was not likely to head along those lines that produce attacks on both sides of the boards, with White launching his assault on the king's side and Black on the queen's.

Black spent little time on the opening, indicating that it had been well prepared, and even the sacrifice of the pawn (13 . . . P-QR4; 14 P-K5, PxP; 15 PxP, N-Q2; 16 NxP, N-B4) was apparently part of the line carefully worked out, a line that gave Black a dangerous attack.

With 18 . . . Q-N4 Black avoided an exchange of queens, which would have been disadvantageous, and posed direct king-side threats, the most direct and obvious being mate at White's KN2. The move served another purpose, too: attacking the vulnerable king pawn. White met both threats adequately with Q-K2.

The move 21 . . . P-R4 signalled that Black was, though now starting to feel the pinch of time, carrying through his original intention of attacking on the king's side. Black carried this theme through the next several moves and, with 27 . . . B-B4, forced White to place his knight in an ineffective position. But then, perhaps unable to work through the complications because of the pressure of time, Black failed to follow through as he should have.

Spassky had taken half an hour on his 18th move

BLACK/SPASSKY

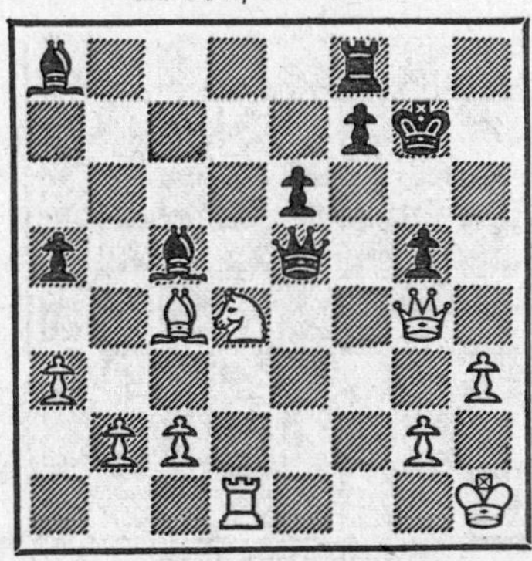

WHITE/FISCHER

29 N-Q4

and even longer on his 19th. Now this consumption of time began to take its toll. The champion played 29 . . . R-R1.

This move turned what could have been a brilliant victory into a draw, for it gave Fischer time to retrench and simplify, taking the impetus out of Spassky's attack and blunting the power of the two bishops that had been pointed menacingly at the threatened king's side.

Fischer played 30 N-B3 and this was followed by 30 . . . BxN; 31 QxB, B-Q3 and then 32 Q-QB3, forcing the exchange of queens by the pin. Fischer, of course, was not totally free during this time, either. Black's 31 . . . B-Q3 posed an immediate threat of mate at KR2, so the reply 32 Q-QB3 was necessary. (Naturally not 32 P-N3, because of the devastating 32 . . . RxPch; and 32 K-N1, in an attempt to open the doors, could have been met by 32 . . . R-R5.)

Had Spassky played 29 . . . R-Q1, instead of 29 . . . R-R1, the continuation could have been 30 P-B3 (forced, to block the crucial square for the pin) and then 30 . . . R-R1; 31 N-B3, BxN; 32 QxB, B-Q3; 33 K-N1. White would have had no alternatives, and this sequence could have been followed by . . . R-R5, threatening . . . Q-R7ch and . . . R-B5, win-

BLACK/SPASSKY

WHITE/FISCHER

Final Position

ning the queen. White could not have played 35 R-Q4 because . . . B-B4, pinning the rook, would have won the exchange and the game.

What followed after the exchange of queens was a further consolidation by White. Fischer is unexcelled as an end-game technician and, with neither side having any material or positional advantage, the draw became inevitable.

Following are the moves of the fourth game:

White Fischer	Black Spassky	White Fischer	Black Spassky
1 P-K4	P-QB4	24 P-R3	B-K6
2 N-KB3	P-Q3	25 Q-N4	QxP
3 P-Q4	PxP	26 QxRP	P-N4
4 NxP	N-KB3	27 Q-N4	B-B4
5 N-QB3	N-B3	28 N-N5	K-N2
6 B-QB4	P-K3	29 N-Q4	R-KR1
7 B-QN3	B-K2	30 N-B3	BxN
8 B-K3	O-O	31 QxB	B-Q3
9 O-O	P-QR3	32 Q-QB3	QxQ
10 P-B4	NxN	33 PxQ	B-K4
11 BxN	P-QN4	34 R-Q7	K-B3
12 P-QR3	B-N2	35 K-N1	BxP
13 Q-Q3	P-QR4	36 B-K2	B-K4
14 P-K5	PxP	37 K-B1	R-QB1
15 PxP	N-Q2	38 B-R5	R-B2
16 NxP	N-B4	39 RxR	BxR
17 BxN	BxBch	40 P-QR4	K-K2
18 K-R1	Q-N4	41 K-K2	P-B4
19 Q-K2	QR-Q1	42 K-Q3	B-K4
20 QR-Q1	RxR	43 P-B4	K-Q3
21 RxR	P-R4	44 B-B7	B-N6
22 N-Q6	B-R1	45 P-B5ch	
23 B-B4	P-KR5	Drawn	

SCORE: Spassky 2½ Fischer 1½

Game Five

The fifth game opened, like the first, with a variation of the Nimzo-Indian Defense. The first 10 moves offered nothing startling or new—the debut has been seen countless times.

On his 11th turn, Spassky, White, used up precious time and came up with P-B4, which offered the possibility of opening up lines. Black, however, declined to go along with that idea and played, instead of 11 . . . PxP, the move 11 . . . N-N3, which kept the position tight.

That was, in general, the theme for the next several moves: White seeking ways to open up the game, Black keeping it closed.

Spassky's play was curiously passive and he failed to play aggressively enough even to retain the initiative. It may well have been that he was worried because he had fared so badly in the third game—which Fischer won even though he played Black—and because he had failed to find the winning line in the fourth game, despite his beautiful attacking position.

Beginning with the 19th move, QR-KB2, White shifted his focus to the king side. With that move and with 20 B-B2 and 21 B-Q2, White lost all momentum and any chance for effective counterplay on the queen's wing.

For his part, Black made the most of White's weaknesses, especially the awkward placement of White's forces. Even if Spassky had not blundered later, he stood no more than an even chance of drawing in an end game, for he had given himself too many weak pawns.

With 23 . . . N-R4 (another of those curious-looking knight moves that Fischer seems to come up with, that cause head-scratching among the experts and tongue-clucking among the less-than-experts and that seem to produce near-magical results) Black forced White's hand. White responded with an exchange of rooks: 24 RxRch, RxR; 25 RxRch, KxR.

Black followed through with 26 . . . N-B5, posting his active and aggressive knight in an outpost from which all sorts of threats could be developed.

White, pressed for time, now made a colossal blunder; he played 27 Q-B2?? It is rare for such a gross error to be made in grandmaster play, and in championship play it is virtually unknown.

BLACK/FISCHER

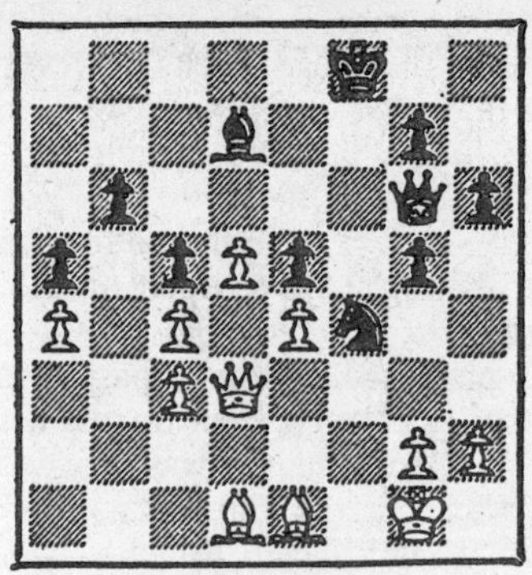

WHITE/SPASSKY

26 . . . N-B5

Black pounced on the error, playing 27 . . . BxP, an X-ray attack that was beyond refutation. Had Spassky captured the bishop with his queen, Fischer could have taken the White king pawn with his queen, threatening immediate mate, with the capture by the queen of the pawn at White's KN2.

The White queen, had it captured the Black bishop, could not have returned in time to the king's side of the board to prevent the mayhem.

Did White have an alternative at his 27th move? It seems doubtful if anything could have helped much. The move 27 Q-N1 could have prolonged the game perhaps, but it could not, in the long run have prevented Black's victory.

Spassky's difficulty, in this game as in others, lay not only in his curiously lackluster play, but also in his strangely profligate use of time. He ran into time trouble early and the press of time only grew worse. Finally, it told in his having made that inexplicable blunder. At the end, he had used 2 hours and 11 minutes (had the game not ended abruptly, he would have had to make 13 moves in 29 minutes!) to Fischer's 1 hour and 18 minutes.

BLACK/FISCHER

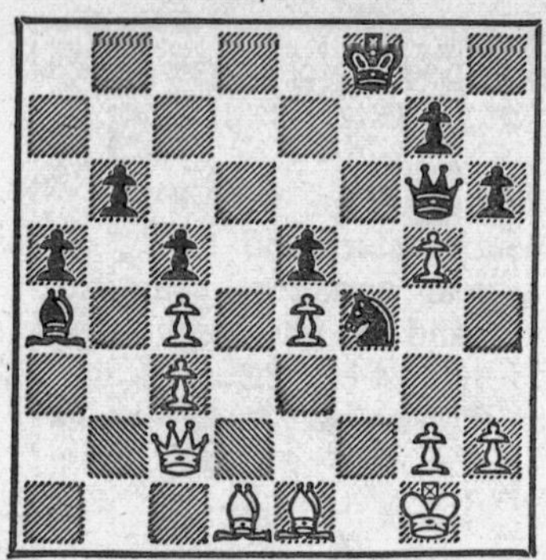

WHITE/SPASSKY

Final Position

Following are the moves of the fifth game:

White Spassky	Black Fischer	White Spassky	Black Fischer
1 P-Q4	N-KB3	15 O-O	O-O
2 P-QB4	P-K3	16 P-QR4	P-QR4
3 N-QB3	B-QN5	17 R-N1	B-Q2
4 N-KB3	P-QB4	18 R-N2	R-N1
5 P-K3	N-QB3	19 QR-KB2	Q-K2
6 B-Q3	BxNch	20 B-B2	P-KN4
7 PxB	P-Q3	21 B-Q2	Q-K1
8 P-K4	P-K4	22 B-K1	Q-N3
9 P-Q5	N-K2	23 Q-Q3	N-R4
10 N-R4	P-KR3	24 RxRch	RxR
11 P-B4	N-N3	25 RxRch	KxR
12 NxN	PxN	26 B-Q1	N-B5
13 PxP	PxP	27 Q-B2??	BxP
14 B-K3	P-N3	Resigns	

SCORE: Spassky 2½ Fischer 2½

Game Six

The sixth game of the world championship match offered something of a rare gem—an opening played to perfection.

It began with a startling surprise: a queen's pawn opening by Fischer. The challenger had played some 750 tournament and match games in his career and in all but three of those games he had used the opening 1 P-K4.

Fischer followed an analysis that had been prepared by Soviet masters and that had been published more than a year earlier. Presumably, Spassky was familiar with it, and the champion also was believed to be one of the foremost exponents of the Queen's Gambit Declined. But Fischer outplayed him every step of the way.

Once more, Spassky played in passive fashion—in such passive fashion, in fact, that it is hard to say at what point exactly he went wrong. Fischer, on the other hand, kept applying more and more pressure, working up what Wilhelm Steinitz, the 19th-century world champion, called "an accumulation of small advantages."

On his 13th move, White played Q-R3, dividing his opponent's play into halves of the board—the king's side and the queen's side—and pinned down movements on the queen's side so that he could force weaknesses in its structure. Then, no matter how Black played, White in the long run could take advantage of the vulnerable set-up.

The line, a strong one, is well known, and Spassky had played it himself many times before on the black side. Yet he continued to play passively.

Then came White's powerful 14 B-N5, which took the game away from the well-beaten path. It also kept Black from stealing the initiative, which had happened in the third and fifth games.

With the sequence 19 NxB, PxN; 20 P-K4 White made his intentions clear (though there really was little doubt all along). This was a sharp thrust in the center that could not safely be met with a passive reply.

Black did reply strongly, but the move, 20 . . . P-Q5, weakened the white squares. Still, there were no other viable alternatives.

White now pressed his advantage, playing 21 P-B4, confirming his control in the center and threatening

BLACK/SPASSKY

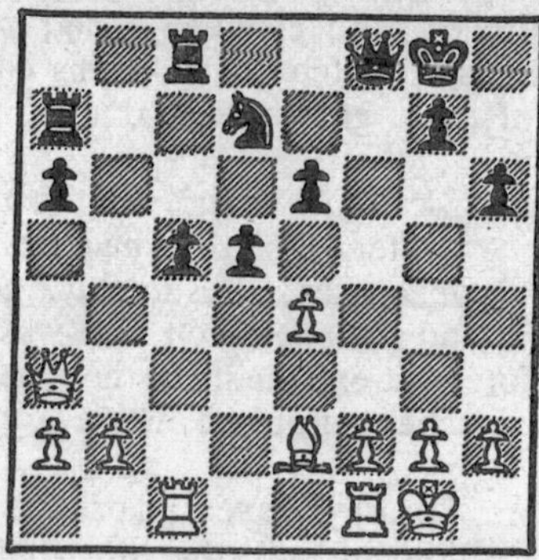

WHITE/FISCHER

20 P-K4

B-B4. The pressure was, at this point, beginning to build up. For the next several moves, White consolidated his position, bringing his pieces into active, closely joined cooperation.

With 28 QR-B1 and 29 Q-N3 White began weaving a powerful mating net. Black's passive play earlier had made this possible, and now there was no time left for shoring up the weaknesses left by that passive play.

Black did what little he could, but the pressure kept building up. The White bishop at B4, the rooks staring down the king bishop file and the queen poised for movement and attack presented an overwhelming threat.

The beginning of the end came with White's sacrifice of the exchange— 38 RxN, PxR; 39 RxP.

The attack was overwhelming. There was nothing Black could do to prevent the onslaught.

The finale was 40 B-B4, K-R1; 41 Q-B4. Mate was inevitable, and Black resigned.

Many seemed to think that, in this game especially, Fischer's play matched that of Capablanca. In many respects, of course, there was a similarity. For one thing, Capablanca maintained an air of invincibility; for another, he maintained a winning streak without losing a game in 10 years.

BLACK/SPASSKY

WHITE/FISCHER

Final Position

But above all, the similarity lay in the simplicity and classic beauty of the play. Many people used to think they could understand Capablanca's chess because it was so simply expressed. And many today feel the same about Fischer's games. Fischer, it is felt, is finding the same kind of profound yet simple moves that Capablanca used to make.

Following are the moves of the sixth game:

White Fischer	Black Spassky	White Fischer	Black Spassky
1 P-QB4	P-K3	18 N-Q4	Q-B1
2 N-KB3	P-Q4	19 NxB	PxN
3 P-Q4	N-KB3	20 P-K4	P-Q5
4 N-B3	B-K2	21 P-KB4	Q-K2
5 B-N5	O-O	22 P-K5	R-N1
6 P-K3	P-KR3	23 B-B4	K-R1
7 B-R4	P-QN3	24 Q-R3	N-B1
8 PxP	NxP	25 P-QN3	P-QR4
9 BxB	QxB	26 P-B5	PxP
10 NxN	PxN	27 RxP	N-R2
11 R-B1	B-K3	28 QR-B1	Q-Q1
12 Q-R4	P-QB4	29 Q-N3	R-K2
13 Q-R3	R-B1	30 P-KR4	R/N1-N2
14 B-N5	P-QR3	31 P-K6	R/N2-B2
15 PxP	PxP	32 Q-K5	Q-K1
16 O-O	R-R2	33 P-QR4	Q-Q1
17 B-K2	N-Q2	34 R/1-B2	Q-K1

White Fischer	Black Spassky	White Fischer	Black Spassky
35 R/2-B3	Q-Q1	39 RxP	K-N1
36 B-Q3	Q-K1	40 B-B4	K-R1
37 Q-K4	N-B3	41 Q-B4	Resigns
38 RxN	PxR		

SCORE: Spassky 2½ Fischer 3½

Game Seven

It was Spassky's turn, in the seventh game, to begin with a surprise. He opened with the king pawn, which was as unexpected as Fischer's opening with the queen bishop pawn in the previous game.

Fischer, playing Black, replied with his favorite king-pawn defense, the Sicilian, characterized by 1 . . . P-QB4. This is a fighting game, and that first Black move says that passive play is not going to be the theme.

Black continued in that vein, adopting, with 5 . . . P-QR3, the Najdorf line, one of his favorites (and he is generally felt to be the greatest exponent of the line). But this time Spassky, playing White, indicated that he, too, was not prepared to play passively. His 6 B-KN5 is a sharp and aggressive line.

The game continued with 6 . . . P-K3; 7 P-B4, Q-N3; 8 Q-Q2, QxP —the so-called "poisoned pawn" variation. Fischer had used it before, and successfully, and he had grabbed a different "poisoned pawn" in the first game, with unsuccessful results.

At any rate, those first eight moves signaled: "fireworks ahead."

White's reply, 9 N-N3, is the first move in what can become a trap for the invading queen. Careful play is required on Black's part to keep his queen from falling into the trap, which can be closed, for example, with P-QR3 and R-R2.

With his 10th move, . . . B-K2, Fischer deviated from the variation analyzed by Soviet grandmasters, who advocated 10 QN-Q2. The line he chose tended to consolidate his king side more effectively.

White then seemed under pressure to sacrifice a second pawn to maintain the initiative—a dangerous continuation at best.

On his 15th move, White played B-N5ch. He could have tried, instead, 15 Q-B4, which could have led to the sacrifice of a piece and a very dangerous attack. But no clearly winning lines were found in this variation, and a dangerous attack is not the same as a winning one, especially when a piece has been sacrificed for it.

Black replied 15 . . . PxB and, after 16 NxPch, K-B1; 17 NxB, White had taken the black bishop to bring the material even. However, Spassky had used more than half an hour more than Fischer and was—as usual—behind in time.

At his 18th move, Spassky again had a choice: instead of 18 N-Q6, by which he hoped to force an end game with drawing chances, he could have tried 18 Q-Q7, keeping up the pressure. But by this time he had 58 minutes more on his clock than Fischer had, and prudence began to play more of a part in his decisions.

Fischer, however, declined to trade queens. Continuing forcefully, he tried to bring about an end game of his own choosing that seemed to hold good promise of victory. Spassky—despite the time pressure—managed to maintain aggressive play and improve his position.

And Fischer, moreover, seemed to miss a more promising continuation. He played 30 . . . B-B4, when he could have played 30 . . . K-N3, which would have preserved the strong bishop.

Spassky spent 40 minutes thinking about his sealed 41st move and, at adjournment, it was difficult to assess the chances.

The move that Spassky sealed at adjournment, 41 P-KR4, is generally felt to have been the only correct move, for it was the key to holding the precarious position. The move 41 R-Q5 could have been followed by 41 . . . P-B3; 42 P-R4, R-B6, with a winning game for Black.

If Spassky found the only correct continuation, Fischer, on the other hand, apparently missed the best

BLACK/FISCHER

WHITE/SPASSKY

40 . . . K-N3

line when he played 43 . . . K-B4. Had he played 43 . . . RxN —sacrificing an inactive rook for the knight—he could have had winning chances.

The move 43 . . . RxN could have been followed by 44 RxR, N-Q2, threatening . . . N-B6ch and . . . P-N6, with inevitable mate. To prevent this, Spassky would have had to move his king to the second rank, allowing a discovered check, with the subsequent loss of the king rook pawn.

BLACK/FISCHER

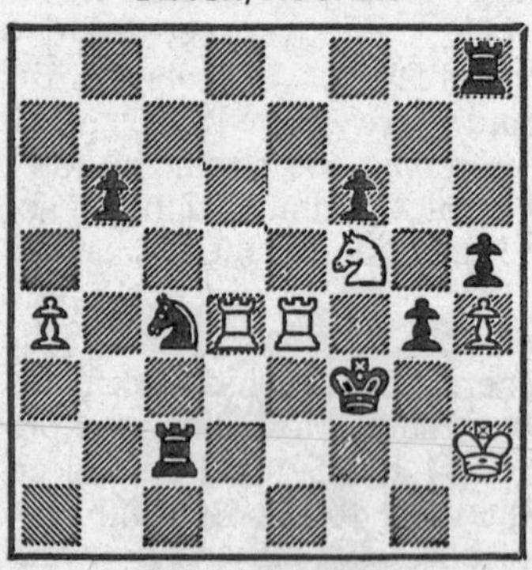

WHITE/SPASSKY

Final Position

In certain variations, the black rook could have moved to KR5, creating passed pawns that could have made serious trouble for Spassky.

The game in at least one sense was a curiosity: Black's king rook remained on its original square throughout. In the end, Fischer was, in effect, operating with a rook less than Spassky.

Following are the moves of the seventh game:

White Spassky	Black Fischer	White Spassky	Black Fischer
1 P-K4	P-QB4	26 QxQ	NxQ
2 N-KB3	P-Q3	27 R-K2	K-N2
3 P-Q4	PxP	28 N-R5	P-N3
4 NxP	N-KB3	29 N-B4	N-Q4
5 N-QB3	P-QR3	30 N/B4-Q6	B-B4
6 B-KN5	P-K3	31 N-N7	R-QB1
7 P-KB4	Q-N3	32 P-B4	N-K6
8 Q-Q2	QxP	33 R-B3	NxP
9 N-N3	Q-R6	34 PxP	P-N5
10 B-Q3	B-K2	35 R-Q3	P-R4
11 O-O	P-R3	36 P-R3	N-R4
12 B-R4	NxP	37 N/7-Q6	BxN
13 NxN	BxB	38 NxB	R-B8ch
14 P-B5	PxP	39 K-N2	N-B5
15 B-N5ch	PxB	40 N-K8ch	K-N3
16 NxPch	K-B1	41 P-R4	P-B3
17 NxB	N-B3	42 R-K6	R-B7ch
18 N-Q6	R-Q1	43 K-N1	K-B4
19 NxP/N5	Q-K2	44 N-N7ch	KxP
20 Q-B4	P-KN3	45 R-Q4ch	K-N6
21 P-R4	B-N4	46 N-B5ch	K-B6
22 Q-B4	B-K6ch	47 R/6-K4	R-B8ch
23 K-R1	P-B5	48 K-R2	R-B7ch
24 P-N3	P-N4	49 K-N1	
25 QR-K1	Q-N5	Drawn	

SCORE: Spassky 3 Fischer 4

Game Eight

The eighth game was a disaster for Spassky. Fischer, playing White, not only decisively defeated him, he also even toyed with the champion for a while, like a cat with a mouse.

The first nine moves of an English Opening went easily enough, and nothing startling developed. But then Fischer played 10 B-N5, instead of the better-known 10 Q-Q3, and followed up with 11 Q-B4, cramping Black on the king's wing and exerting pressure through the center.

Eventually, the game transposed back to the variation involving 10 Q-Q3, but Spassky picked up an extra tempo because Fischer had first moved his bishop to N5 and then back to K3.

Spassky might have obtained the better game by preparing to double his rooks on the queen bishop file on the 15th move, playing 15 . . . R-B2 instead of the doubtful exchange sacrifice he offered with 15 . . . P-QN4. But Black apparently was counting on his extra tempo to help him out.

The tempo, apparently, was not worth the exchange, even with the initial two-pawn advantage that went along with it.

The game might still have been tenable for Black had he not allowed White to win the king's pawn by playing 20 N-Q5. Spassky's 19 . . . N-Q2 was, therefore, a bad mistake, incomprehensible in championship-level competition. Almost any alternative that could have prevented the subsequent intermezzo check—such

BLACK/SPASSKY

WHITE/FISCHER

15 . . . P-QN4

as 19 . . . Q-Q1 or 19 . . . K-B1 —would have been better.

Black's blunder was not overlooked by White, who played 20 N-Q5, QxQ; 21 NxPch.

At that point Black had not only lost the exchange, but also had nothing to show for it, for White had regained the pawns.

At that point, too, Black might just as well have resigned, for he had an irretrievably lost game. Only a catastrophic blunder by White could have saved Black, and Fischer is not known for making catastrophic blunders.

The position was so hopeless that most experts lost interest in the game and did not even stay to see the last 17 moves, or to analyze them later.

BLACK/SPASSKY

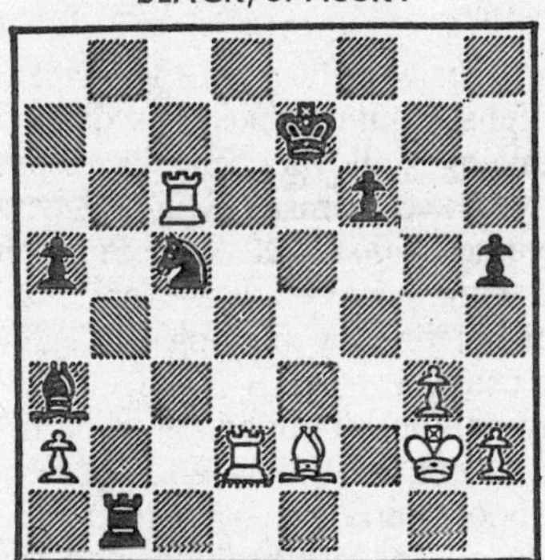

WHITE/FISCHER

Final Position

Following are the moves of the eighth game:

White Fischer	Black Spassky	White Fischer	Black Spassky
1 P-QB4	P-QB4	7 P-Q4	PxP
2 N-QB3	N-QB3	8 NxP	NxN
3 N-B3	N-B3	9 QxN	P-Q3
4 P-KN3	P-KN3	10 B-N5	B-K3
5 B-N2	B-N2	11 Q-B4	Q-R4
6 O-O	O-O	12 QR-QB1	QR-N1

White Fischer	Black Spassky	White Fischer	Black Spassky
13 P-N3	KR B1	26 P-K4	B-R8
14 Q-Q2	P-QR3	27 P-B4	P-B3
15 B-K3	P-QN4	28 R-K2	K-K3
16 B-R7	PxP	29 R/2-QB2	B-N7
17 BxR	RxB	30 B-K2	P-R4
18 PxP	BxP	31 R-Q2	B-R6
19 KR-Q1	N-Q2	32 P-B5ch	PxP
20 N-Q5	QxQ	33 PxPch	K-K4
21 NxPch	K-B1	34 R/4-Q4	KxP
22 RxQ	KxN	35 R-Q5ch	K-K3
23 RxB	R-N8ch	36 RxPch	K-K2
24 B-B1	N-B4	37 R-QB6	Resigns
25 K-N2	P-QR4		

SCORE: Spassky 3 Fischer 5

Game Nine

In the ninth game, Fischer, on the black side, chose a Tarrasch Defense against Spassky's queen's gambit.

The challenger allowed Spassky to play a variation that Fischer had used himself—and successfully—in his fifth match game against Petrosian in Buenos Aires.

On the eighth move, however, Fischer deviated from the normal line by playing . . . N-QB3 instead of the more usual 8 . . . B-N5ch.

The champion responded by playing a move that fits into the system, 9 B-QB4 and that could have led back to the book variation by transposition if Fischer had chosen to do so, by checking with the bishop and exchanging it, followed by castling and then . . . P-QN3 and . . . B-N2.

Instead, however, after thinking for about 20 minutes, Fischer decided to play an aggressive move that took Spassky right out of known theory. His ninth move, 9 . . . P-QN4, does weaken Black's queen side, but the game seems to prove that Black has sufficient counter-pressure against White's queen pawn to equalize.

The knight pawn, of course, could not be taken because of the possibility of . . . Q-R4ch and the subsequent capture of the white bishop by the black queen.

BLACK/FISCHER

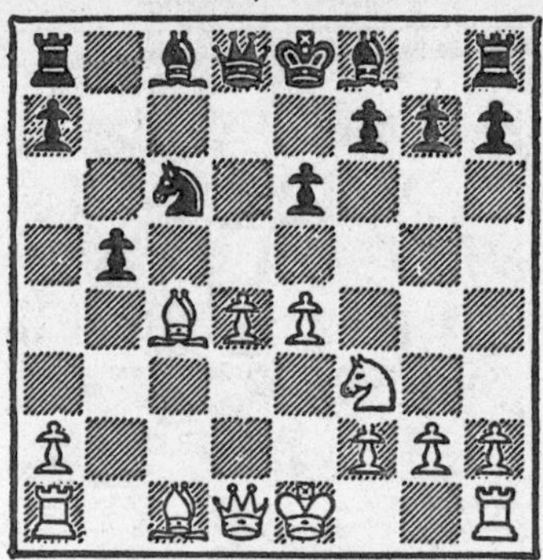

WHITE/SPASSKY

9 . . . P-QN4

After Black's unorthodox ninth move, White spent much time considering possible refutations of the early push by the black queen knight pawn. There was the possibility of playing P-QR4 before castling. White eventually played this, and the game demonstrated that this idea does not prevent Black from obtaining an even game.

Instead of 13 P-QR4, White might have tried 13 PxP, but this could have been followed by 13 . . . NxP; 14 NxN, QxN, giving Black a slightly better game.

A critical position arose after Black's 17 . . . P-N5.

White's response to this was 18 Q-Q2. Spassky seemed to realize that there was little chance of preventing a situation in which his queen pawn would be exchanged against Fischer's passed queen knight pawn.

One possible continuation was 18 P-Q5, which is similar to the successful strategy used in the fifth Fischer-Petrosian match game. In this game, however, the result probably would have been no better than it actually turned out to be. That move, for example, could have led to the sequence 18 . . . PxP; 19 PxP, PxQ; 20 RxQ, N-R4; 21 P-Q6, etc.

Sooner or later, the advanced pawns would have been mutually exchanged in this variation, too.

BLACK/FISCHER

WHITE/SPASSKY

Final Position

In the actual play, the simplification came about just as quickly, leaving a dead-drawn rook ending with three pawns on each side.

Spassky made a desperate attempt to produce complications in a position that contained none. He offered his rook pawn on the 28th move with 28 P-R4, but Fischer played 28 . . . P-R3, declining it, and a draw was agreed upon two moves later.

Following are the moves of the ninth game:

White Spassky	Black Fischer	White Spassky	Black Fischer
1 P-Q4	N-KB3	16 O-O	Q-N3
2 P-QB4	P-K3	17 QR-N1	P-N5
3 N-KB3	P-Q4	18 Q-Q2	NxP
4 N-B3	P-B4	19 NxN	QxN
5 BPxP	NxP	20 RxP	Q-Q2
6 P-K4	NxN	21 Q-K3	KR-Q1
7 PxN	PxP	22 KR-N1	QxB
8 PxP	N-B3	23 QxQ	RxQ
9 B-QB4	P-QN4	24 RxB	P-N4
10 B-Q3	B-N5ch	25 R-N8ch	RxR
11 B-Q2	BxBch	26 RxRch	K-N2
12 QxB	P-QR3	27 P-B3	R-Q7
13 P-QR4	O-O	28 P-R4	P-R3
14 Q-B3	B-N2	29 PxP	PxP
15 PxP	PxP	Drawn	

SCORE: Spassky 3½ Fischer 5½

Game Ten

With the 10th game Fischer returned to the opening move that had become his trademark (and that in some circles was spoken of as a move on which Fischer held a copyright)—P-K4.

Black's reply, 1 . . . P-K4, permitted the game to move into one of the oldest and best-analyzed openings in the chess literature, the Ruy Lopez.

What followed then was 2 N-KB3, N-QB3; 3 B-N5, P-QR3; 4 B-R4, N-B3; 5 O-O, B-K2; 6 R-K1, P-QN4; 7 B-N3, P-Q3; 8 P-KR3, O-O; 9 P-B3, N-N1. This is the Breyer line, one of Spassky's favorites, and the champion emerged from the opening with active play.

But then he fell down, and it is difficult to pinpoint with any accuracy just where he went wrong, where he might have played more accurately and come out with better results.

One such possibility arose on the 22d move, when Black could have captured the bishop with the pawn instead of with the queen. This might have weakened Black's king side, but it might have nonetheless retained the initiative for him.

Another possible chance occurred when Black decided to take the queen rook pawn on the 25th move. After this, White opened a strong attack that eventually led to the win of the exchange for a pawn. Black might have been better off playing 25 . . . PxP.

The game had already begun to deteriorate for Spassky, but it might yet have been steered along profitable channels even as late as the 29th move. Instead of . . . R-K2, Black might have tried, say, 29 . . . QR-Q1, and this could have been followed by a sequence such as 30 BxPch, RxB; 31 QxRch, QxQ; 32 NxQ, with possibilities of pressing an attack.

The most dramatic variation was threatened by Fischer after 30 BxPch. Had Black replied with 30 . . . K-R1 White could have had a mate in two: 31 N-N6ch, PxN; 32 Q-R4 mate.

BLACK/SPASSKY

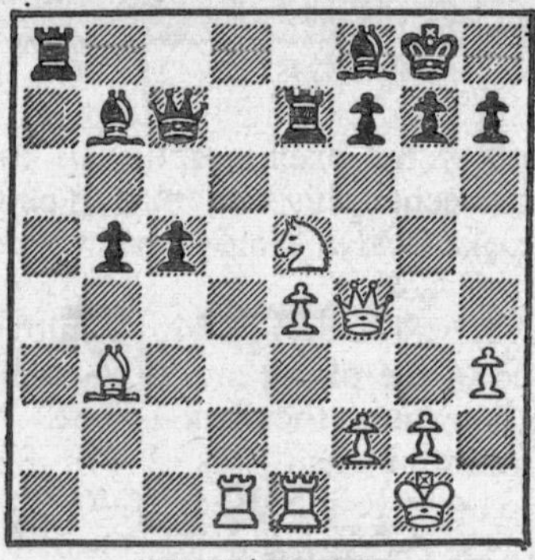

WHITE/FISCHER

29 . . . R-K2

Spassky's two united passed pawns on the queen's wing, which looked so threatening and seemed to offer such excellent chances, turned out to be hollow threats. The pawns were immobilized. Black had lost the exchange in warding off an immediate threat of checkmate, and, at adjournment, the game looked grim for him.

With the resumption of the game, Spassky had to

BLACK/SPASSKY

WHITE/FISCHER

Final Position

allow Fischer to obtain a passed pawn on the king's bishop file, and Fischer also soon picked up one of the two passed pawns Spassky had on the queen's wing.

Spassky was, eventually, left with nothing to show for his loss of the exchange.

When Fischer played his 56th move, R-N1, Spassky had to resign. Had the game continued, it might have run like this: 56 . . . BxP; 58 R-Q1ch, K-B5; 58 RxPch, KxR; 59 RxR, leaving White with a rook and pawn for the lone black bishop.

Since a bishop and king cannot force mate, Spassky would have had absolutely no chance to win; his only hope—a virtually nonexistent one—would have been for Fischer to slip and permit a stalemate.

Following are the moves of the 10th game:

White Fischer	Black Spassky	White Fischer	Black Spassky
1 P-K4	P-K4	29 QR-Q1	R-K2
2 N-KB3	N-QB3	30 BxPch	RxB
3 B-N5	P-QR3	31 QxRch	QxQ
4 B-R4	N-B3	32 NxQ	BxP
5 O-O	B-K2	33 RxB	KxN
6 R-K1	P-QN4	34 R-Q7ch	K-B3
7 B-N3	P-Q3	35 R-N7	R-R8ch
8 P-KR3	O-O	36 K-R2	B-Q3ch
9 P-B3	N-N1	37 P-N3	P-N5
10 P-Q4	QN-Q2	38 K-N2	P-R4
11 QN-Q2	B-N2	39 R-N6	R-Q3
12 B-B2	R-K1	40 K-B3	K-B2
13 P-QN4	B-KB1	41 K-K2	R-Q4
14 P-QR4	N-N3	42 P-B4	P-N3
15 P-R5	QN-Q2	43 P-N4	PxP
16 B-N2	Q-N1	44 PxP	P-N4
17 R-N1	P-B4	45 P-B5	B-K4
18 NPxP	PxBP	46 R-N5	K-B3
19 PxKP	N/2xP	47 R(4)xP	B-Q5
20 NxN	QxN	48 R-N6ch	K-K4
21 P-QB4	Q-B5	49 K-B3	R-Q1
22 BxN	QxB	50 R-N8	R-Q2
23 PxP	KR-Q1	51 R(5)-N7	R-Q3
24 Q-B1	Q-QB6	52 R-N6	R-Q2
25 N-B3	QxP	53 R-KN6	K-Q4
26 B-N3	PxP	54 RxP	B-K4
27 Q-KB4	R-Q2	55 P-B6	K-Q5
28 N-K5	Q-B2	56 R-N1	Resigns

SCORE: Spassky 3½ Fischer 6½

Game Eleven

The 11th game was an exciting and dramatic one in which the eternal question of the "poisoned pawn" arose again and the old saw about "he who grabs the queen knight's pawn sleeps in the streets" had some new life pumped into it.

Spassky, almost hopelessly behind in match points, opened with 1 P-K4, signaling that he was going to keep fighting and not just lie back and die.

The first few moves followed the course of the seventh game, which—after Fischer grabbed the "poisoned" queen knight pawn—wound up in a draw. As he did then, Fischer grabbed that pawn on his eighth move and, as he did in that earlier game, Spassky replied by bringing his knight over to his N3, starting to close the trap on the invading queen.

If nothing else, White can gain tempi in attacking the queen, for Black must lose precious time in retreating his biggest weapon.

This time, Fischer allowed Spassky to break up his king-side pawn structure, and this line brought approval from grandmasters who called it "much more logical, much sharper," than the earlier game.

In professional chess circles, any defense given a second try within a few days is always suspect, and the chances of its being played are almost zero. But Fischer has so much confidence in himself (and so little in others) that he is hardly willing to believe that something he has passed by as being faulty needs to be analyzed again.

Thus he tempted fate again with the "poisoned pawn" grab. Before he realized it, he had fallen into the trap. The move 14 N-N1, which seemingly was a time-waster, actually was a good one that forced Fischer's attention. It limited the scope of his queen, and opened up new lines. Perhaps its greatest asset for Spassky was its unexpectedness.

Black replied 14 . . . Q-N5 (naturally not 14 . . . Q-N7, which could have been rebutted with

BLACK/FISCHER

WHITE/SPASSKY

24 . . . P-R6

15 P-QR3), trying to keep his queen from becoming ensnared.

Superficially, Black's reply of 16 . . . N-K2 to White's 16 PxP seemed to give Black sufficient action for his pieces to promote a new initiative.

The Black knight, now scheduled for B4 or possibly N6, coupled with the diagonals commanded by the bishop and castling on the queen's side, seemed to promise a lasting attack. Even as late as 23 Q-QB3 it seemed that Black was going to survive with a powerful end game.

But this was not to be, because White was able to trade off the reserves and take the force out of any potential Black attack.

Black attempted to press a pair of pawns, backed up by a rook, as a king-side threat. But his inability to bring other forces to bear on the position, to back up the forward pawns with heavy pieces, spelled his doom.

Perhaps with long study Fischer would have been able to cope with the variation as played in the end game. But, on short notice, he obviously was not up to it.

With 24 . . . P-R6 he attempted to do the impossible—use his pawn wedge to pry open the white king's defenses. But White never gave him time to do this.

With 26 KxP, White effectively shattered any thin hopes Black might still have been harboring. Then came the crushing ending: 27 Q-B6, N-B4; 28 P-B6, B-B1; 29 PxKP, PxKP; 30 KR-K1, B-K2; 31 RxKP.

There was nothing left for Black to do but resign.

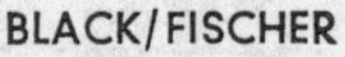

WHITE/SPASSKY

Final Position

Following are the moves of the eleventh game:

White Spassky	Black Fischer	White Spassky	Black Fischer
1 P-K4	P-QB4	17 P-B4	N-B4
2 N-KB3	P-Q3	18 Q-Q3	P-R5
3 P-Q4	PxP	19 B-N4	N-Q3
4 NxP	N-KB3	20 N/1-Q2	P-B4
5 N-QB3	P-QR3	21 P-QR3	Q-N3
6 B-KN5	P-K3	22 P-B5	Q-N4
7 P-B4	Q-N3	23 Q-QB3	PxB
8 Q-Q2	QxP	24 P-R4	P-R6
9 N-N3	Q-R6	25 PxQ	PxPch
10 BxN	PxB	26 KxP	R-R6
11 B-K2	P-KR4	27 Q-B6	N-B4
12 O-O	N-B3	28 P-B6	B-B1
13 K-R1	B-Q2	29 QPxP	BPxP
14 N-N1	Q-N5	30 KR-K1	B-K2
15 Q-K3	P-Q4	31 KRxP	Resigns
16 PxP	N-K2		

SCORE: Spassky 4½ Fischer 6½

Game Twelve

After the tactically exciting and dramatic 11th game, the 12th game was something of a quiet intermezzo. It was a positional game in which each player searched for minute advantages, tiny weaknesses in his opponent's structure.

This was unexpected, because it had been felt that Fischer, smarting from the devastating defeat of the previous game, would come out swinging and breathing fire.

As if to refute this, Fischer played almost cautiously, and for the first time in the match, he was behind Spassky on the clock almost to the end of the first part of the game.

The opening was again an Orthodox Defense to the Queen's Gambit. Fischer departed from his standard 1 P-K4 more in this match than he had in his entire previous chess career.

The first several moves went quickly—almost at rapid-transit speed—but Spassky steered the game away from the line that led to his defeat in the sixth game.

By the 11th move the game had become one in which the variation was one Spassky had never been known to use—and it was believed that Fischer had never tried the line either.

Despite the unfamiliarity of the territory, neither player seemed to get lost or to falter. There was constant jockeying, of a delicate sort, back and forth.

With 21 N-B6, B/2xN; 22 BxB, White emerged with the slight advantage of the bishop-pair. For a while it seemed that a draw by repetition of moves was possible, but this possibility disappeared with Fischer's 31 P-N3.

At adjournment, with White having sealed his 41st move, the position seemed just about even, with Fischer's bishop-pair unlikely to bring about any substantial advantage in the relatively simple position on the board.

BLACK/SPASSKY

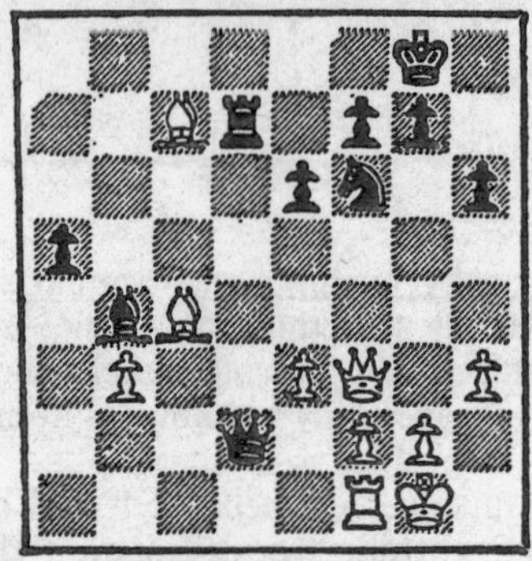

WHITE/FISCHER

40 . . . R-Q2

When the game resumed, the players moved quickly, following lines laid down by the analysts during the night. Fischer's sealed move turned out to be, as expected, 41 Q-B6, and it brought nods of approval from grandmasters.

On the 48th move, R-B1, Fischer offered a draw by repetition. Fischer and Spassky could then have re-

BLACK/SPASSKY

WHITE/FISCHER

Final Position

treated to the previous position, followed by still another repetition of the position.

This time, however, Spassky refused the draw. Several moves later he actually won a pawn, but it made little difference. With bishops of opposite color the situation was what is known as a book draw. Neither player could force a victory and there was no reason to continue.

After the 55th move, Spassky offered a draw—this time by direct offer rather than by repetition of moves—and Fischer accepted it.

Following are the moves of the 12th game:

	White Fischer	Black Spassky		White Fischer	Black Spassky
1	P-QB4	P-K3	29	B-K2	Q-B3
2	N-KB3	P-Q4	30	B-B3	Q-N4
3	P-Q4	N-KB3	31	P-N3	B-K2
4	N-B3	B-K2	32	B-K2	Q-N5
5	B-N5	P-KR3	33	B-R6	R-B3
6	B-R4	O-O	34	B-Q3	N-B4
7	P-K3	QN-Q2	35	Q-B3	R-B1
8	R-B1	P-B3	36	NxN	BxN
9	B-Q3	PxP	37	R-B1	R-Q1
10	BxP	P-QN4	38	B-B4	Q-Q7
11	B-Q3	P-R3	39	R-B1	B-N5
12	P-R4	PxP	40	B-B7	R-Q2
13	NxP	Q-R4ch	41	Q-B6	Q-B7
14	N-Q2	B-N5	42	B-K5	R-Q7
15	N-B3	P-B4	43	Q-R8ch	K-R2
16	N-N3	Q-Q1	44	BxN	PxB
17	O-O	PxP	45	Q-B3	P-B4
18	NxP	B-N2	46	P-N4	Q-K5
19	B-K4	Q-N1	47	K-N2	K-N3
20	B-N3	Q-R2	48	R-B1	B-R6
21	N-B6	B/2xN	49	R-QR1	B-N5
22	BxB	QR-B1	50	R-QB1	B-K2
23	N-R4	KR-Q1	51	PxPch	PxP
24	B-B3	P-QR4	52	R-K1	RxPch
25	R-B6	RxR	53	KxR	B-R5ch
26	BxR	R-QB1	54	K-K2	QxQch
27	B-B3	Q-R3	55	KxQ	BxR
28	P-R3	Q-N4		Drawn	

SCORE: Spassky 5 Fischer 7

Game Thirteen

In the 13th game Spassky, White, opened with his king pawn, as he did in the seventh and 11th games. In the former, he sacrificed three pawns and a bishop for an attack. He did not win the game but he had excellent prospects for the material sacrificed. It was superb defense that saved Fischer in that game.

In the 11th game, Spassky again resorted to the king pawn opening and won brilliantly. It was, therefore, not surprising when he again elected to open with 1 P-K4 in this game, especially in view of the fact that in other games Spassky fared poorly when, as White, he selected the queen pawn opening as his first move.

Fischer's first move was a great surprise. He replied 1 N-KB3, the Alekhine Defense, which, if memory serves, he had never played against a top-level grandmaster.

In fact, the Alekhine Defense had not been used in world championship matches except, perhaps, in one of the games between Alekhine and Euwe in 1936 or 1938.

The reason for Fischer's choice was probably the result of the 11th game. In that encounter, Fischer, playing the Najdorf Variation of the Sicilian Defense, his pet opening, suffered perhaps the worst defeat of his chess career.

It is interesting that both Fischer and Spassky attempted to upset each other psychologically in the choice of openings. Spassky shifted from the queen opening to the king opening, which is not unusual for him. Fischer's action, however, in deviating from the king pawn opening to the queen bishop opening is most astonishing. His opening choice in the 12th game was most astounding. It might be a strong indication that he has not found an adequate defense against Spassky's approach to the Najdorf Variation.

When Fischer fianchettoed his king bishop at N2,

Spassky seemed undecided as to the proper continuation. His followers were not greatly inspired when he spent 20 minutes pondering over his next move.

On his ninth move, Spassky made a dubious move when he advanced his queen rook pawn two squares. The pawn soon became a target for Fischer's knights and queen. Preferable was 9 P-QR3. This was necessary to have a flight square for the bishop at QR2.

After Black's 12 . . . Q-K1, White's queen rook pawn could not be saved. The question was, did Spassky have sufficient compensation for the pawn and did he plan to get into this situation?

It soon became clear that Spassky was going all out for an assault against Fischer's king. Spassky advanced his king side pawns in an attempt to pry open Black's king position at the cost of exposing his own king.

Fischer defended expertly in the middle game, parrying all of Spassky's threats successfully. Fischer forced the exchange of queens, holding on to his extra pawn. Both had dangerous passed pawns.

After Spassky's 37 R-KB1, the threat was R-B4-KR4 with the menacing threat of R-R7ch, harassing Black's king. Fischer's reply of 37 . . . R-R1 was an excellent reply. For if White continued 38 BxR, then

BLACK/FISCHER

WHITE/SPASSKY

37 R-KB1

with 38 . . . RxB, Black could easily dispose of White's passed queen pawn with an easy victory in sight.

At adjournment, after 41 moves, the position appeared simple.

Fischer was expected to increase his advantage gradually without great resistance by his opponent, but Spassky and his aides came up with a fantastic continuation bringing about a tense and exciting struggle. Fischer was faced with problems, but he solved them satisfactorily.

After misplaying the opening and obtaining only an imaginary bind on the position in the middle game, Spassky was fortunate to have even an outside chance to hold his own in the resulting end game.

To appreciate the depth of the adjourned position, it is necessary to be aware of the pros and cons in the position for Fischer and Spassky.

The bishops of opposite colors were in Spassky's favor as far as drawing chances for him were concerned. Fischer's two extra pawns offered him winning chances. In addition, his immediate threat of advancing the queen knight pawn to queen knight five, followed by advancing his queen bishop pawn to queen bishop six, cutting off White's bishop from queen rook one, would enable Black's queen rook pawn to be promoted to a queen.

Spassky, consequently, had to come up with a plan that would keep Fischer busy with immediate threats. This Spassky did when he sealed his 42d move, K-N3, intending 43 R-KR4, and if 43 . . . RxR, 44 KxR, with the result that Black would incur loss of the other rook after P-Q8 (Q).

One the other hand, if Black decided to move his rook on KR1 to any other square, White would continue R-R7ch, with at least a perpetual check.

As a result of prolonged analysis, Fischer found a profound continuation leading to a most complex position when he played 42 . . . R-R6ch. From the rapidity of Spassky's replies it was evident that Spassky's analysts anticipated Black's plan. A most remarkable position arose. Fischer gave up his bishop, for which he had three dangerously connected pawns.

The ensuing play was instructive and precise. Spassky succeeded in forcing Fischer's rook to be completely immobilized, but Fischer was still able to make progress by the coordinated action of his king and advanced pawns. Spassky defended valiantly but was unable to stem Fischer's determined play. Note that after 75 R-B4, Black would win with 75 . . . RxB; 76 RxR, K-K7; 77 R-KB4, P-B8 (Q); 78 RxQ, KxR, and Black's queen knight pawn would queen without difficulty. 75 BxP would lose to 75 . . . R-Q8.

WHITE/SPASSKY

Final Position

Following are the moves of the 13th game:

White Spassky	Black Fischer	White Spassky	Black Fischer
1 P-K4	N-KB3	14 BxN	NxB
2 P-K5	N-Q4	15 R-K1	N-N3
3 P-Q4	P-Q3	16 B-Q2	P-QR5
4 N-KB3	P-KN3	17 B-N5	P-R3
5 B-QB4	N-N3	18 B-R4	B-B4
6 B-N3	B-N2	19 P-KN4	B-K3
7 QN-Q2	O-O	20 N-Q4	B-B5
8 P-KR3	P-QR4	21 Q-Q2	Q-Q2
9 P-QR4	PxP	22 QR-Q1	KR-K1
10 PxP	N-R3	23 P-B4	B-Q4
11 O-O	N-B4	24 N-QB5	Q-B1
12 Q-K2	Q-K1	25 Q-B3	P-K3
13 N-K4	N/3xP	26 K-R2	N-Q2

White Spassky	Black Fischer	White Spassky	Black Fischer
27 N-Q3	P-QB4	52 R-Q7ch	K-R3
28 N-N5	Q-B3	53 R(7)-Q2	RxR
29 N-Q6	QxN	54 KxR	P-N5
30 PxQ	BxQ	55 P-R4	K-N4
31 PxB	P-B3	56 P-R5	P-QB5
32 P-N5	RPxP	57 R-QR1	PxP
33 PxP	P-B4	58 P-N6	P-KR5
34 B-N3	K-B2	59 P-N7	P-R6
35 N-K5ch	NxN	60 B-K7	R-KN1
36 BxN	P-N4	61 B-B8	P-R7
37 R-KB1	R-R1	62 K-B2	K-B3
38 B-B6	P-R6	63 R-Q1	P-N6ch
39 R-B4	P-R7	64 K-B3	P-KR8(Q)
40 P-B4	BxP	65 RxQ	K-Q4
41 P-Q7	B-Q4	66 K-N2	P-B5
42 K-N3	R-R6ch	67 R-Q1ch	K-K5
43 P-QB3	KR-R1	68 R-QB1	K-Q6
44 R-KR4	P-K4	69 R-Q1ch	K-K7
45 R-R7ch	K-K3	70 R-QB1	P-KB6
46 R-K7ch	K-Q6	71 B-B5	RxP
47 RxP	RxPch	72 RxP	R-Q2
48 K-B2	R-B7ch	73 R-K4ch	K-B8
49 K-K1	KxP	74 B-Q4	P-B7
50 R(5)xBch	K-B3	75 Resigns	
51 R-Q6ch	K-N2		

SCORE: Spassky 5 Fischer 8

Game Fourteen

In the 14th game Spassky outplayed Fischer in the middle game, winning a pawn, but the champion threw away his winning chances by committing a blunder on his 27th move, permitting the challenger to equalize.

Fischer, playing White, again kept away from his favorite opening of 1 P-K4, and instead decided on 1 P-QB4. Spassky, as in prior games, replied with 1 . . . P-K3, and a regular queen pawn opening developed.

On his fifth turn, Fischer varied from previous games by continuing with B-KB4, instead of B-KN5.

Several moves later, the opening turned into the well-known Tarrasch Defense, with which Spassky is well acquainted.

On his 12th turn, Fischer wisely discarded the variation in which he could have won a pawn: 12 NxP, NxN; 13 RxB, NxB; 14 PxN, Q-N3, and if 15 Q-B1 (15 R-B2, B-N6) N-Q5, winning material.

Fischer's 13 B-N3 was designed to threaten Spassky's isolated queen pawn, which explains his reply of 13 . . . B-N3.

Spassky could have assured himself of acquiring equality by playing 14 . . . P-Q5, which would have disposed of his weak queen pawn. Indisposed to enter into a clearly drawing line, he elected to continue with 14 . . . N-K2, inviting complications, a clear indication that he was playing for a victory and was unafraid of a real fight.

Spassky's search for a battle in this actionless, open position demonstrates vividly his indomitable fighting spirit. His willingness to undertake risks was all the more remarkable considering his debacle in the 13th game where he threw away the draw on his 69th turn, an extremely depressing and disheartening result.

An intense positional struggle evolved. After the exchange of rooks on the 16th move, some of the middle-game tension diminished. To be able to develop his queen properly, Spassky gave up his queen bishop for Fischer's knight. Posting his queen at his KB3 enabled Spassky to exert pressure on White's queen knight pawn and queen bishop.

After Spassky's 20 . . . Q-B3, Fischer had to contend with two threats by his opponent. First, White's queen knight pawn was attacked. Second, Black was threatening to harass White's queen bishop by continuing 21 . . . P-KN4; 22 B-N3, P-KR4 with the serious threat of trapping the bishop with 23 . . . P-KR5.

Fischer was unable to parry these threats successfully. He therefore decided on giving up the queen knight pawn, reaching an end game after the exchange of queens and hoping that he could survive.

Fischer obviously overlooked Spassky's strong reply of 22 . . . N-B6.

BLACK/SPASSKY

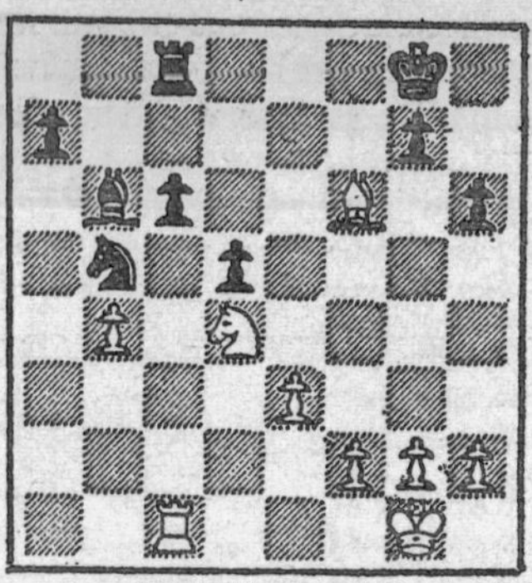

WHITE/FISCHER

27 N-Q4

Just when victory was within his grasp, Spassky made an inexcusable mistake on his 27th turn, playing P-B3. He overlooked a one-move reply that enabled Fischer to regain his pawn, after which a draw was assured for Fischer. The correct move for Spassky was 27 . . . NxN, which could have been followed by 28 BxN, K-B1; 29 BxB, PxB; 30 R-R1, P-QB4; 31 PxP, PxP; 32 K-B1, K-K2, with good winning chances.

BLACK/SPASSKY

WHITE/FISCHER

Final Position

Following are the moves of the 14th game:

White Fischer	Black Spassky	White Fischer	Black Spassky
1 P-QB4	P-K3	22 BxN	N-B6
2 N-KB3	P-Q4	23 Q-N4	QxQ
3 P-Q4	N-KB3	24 PxQ	PxB
4 N-B3	B-K2	25 B-K5	N-N4
5 B-B4	O-O	26 R-B1	R-B1
6 P-K3	P-QB4	27 N-Q4	P-B3
7 PxBP	N-B3	28 BxP	BxN
8 PxQP	PxP	29 BxB	NxB
9 B-K2	BxP	30 PxN	R-N1
10 O-O	B-K3	31 K-B1	RxP
11 R-B1	R-B1	32 RxP	RxP
12 P-QR3	P-KR3	33 R-R6	K-B2
13 B-N3	B-N3	34 RxPch	K-B3
14 N-K5	N-K2	35 R-Q7	P-R4
15 N-R4	N-K5	36 K-K2	P-N4
16 RxR	BxR	37 K-K3	R-K5ch
17 N-KB3	B-Q2	38 K-Q3	K-K3
18 B-K5	BxN	39 R-KN7	K-B3
19 QxB	N-QB3	40 R-Q7	K-K3
20 B-KB4	Q-B3	Drawn	
21 B-QN5	QxP		

SCORE: Spassky 5½ Fischer 8½

Game Fifteen

The 15th game of the world championship chess match was a wild affair. Spassky won a pawn in the opening, which gave him excellent winning chances, but, again, he failed to continue correctly.

Spassky, playing White, decided on P-K4 as his opening move. This was no surprise. The challenger, however, again resorted to psychology by relying on his favorite defense, replying 1 . . . P-QB4, varying from the 13th game, when he chose the Alekhine Defense, in which he outplayed the champion.

Veering away from the "poisoned pawn" variation, Fischer continued 7 . . . B-K2, instead of 7 . . . Q-N3. A well-known line developed.

Chess openings are not static. New moves are always found in accepted lines. New concepts are often introduced. As a result, what is considered at one time as good for one side might become playable or even better for the other side at another time. That is what makes chess the great game it is.

Fischer discarded the obvious 12th move of P-QN5 because of 13 N-Q5, PxN; 14 PxP, with the black monarch subjected to a fierce assault. Fischer would have none of that. Instead, he castled on the queen side. He rejected castling on the king side, on account of 13 P-K5, PxP; 14 PxP, N-R4; 15 Q-R4 with promising pressure against the king's position.

After Fischer's 12th move, a sharp and extremely complicated position arose with numerous possibilities.

Spassky's 13 BxN posed a serious problem for Fischer. If he recaptured the bishop with the knight, White would take his queen.

The Black reply 13 . . . BxB could have led to 14 BxP, PxB (14 . . . BxN; 15 BxNch, followed by 16 RxB, winding up with a pawn to the good) 15 N/Q4x NP, followed by 16 NxPch (after Black's queen moved) with a won position.

Unappetizing was 13 . . . PxB because Black's king bishop would be inactivated, and his pawn structure would be greatly weakened. Fischer took a long time before making up his mind. He finally decided to give up a pawn and continued 13 . . . NxB. It did not appear as if he had obtained sufficient counterplay for the pawn.

Interesting was 16 . . . Q-R4; 17 P-N3, N-R4; 18 Q-K3, and if 18 . . . NxP; 19 BxP! (not 19 QxN, B-N4, winning the queen) BxB (19 . . . QxB, QxN) 20 N-B6, regaining the piece.

Fischer rejected the line in which he would regain a pawn by playing 18 . . . N-B4. There would follow 19 NxN, PxN; 20 N-B3, QxP; 21 Q-K2, P-QR4; 22 P-K5 with good prospects.

Unfavorable for Black would be 20 . . . NxN; 21 BxN, Q-R4; 22 B-B6, PxP; 23 BxB, KxB; 24 R-QB1, and Black's king would be dangerously exposed.

Note that if Black had played 24 . . . BxP, White

could play 25 N/4-N5, PxN; 26 NxNP, Q-N3; 27 RxB, with a won position.

Spassky's 23 P-K5 proved premature, freeing Fischer's pieces for active play. The champion's 29 QxRP was too ambitious, permitting the challenger to obtain a dangerous attack.

In the ensuing wild complications, the champion was on the defensive, and only his great resourcefulness saved him from immediate defeat.

Spassky's 29 QxRP was questionable. A strong alternative for Black was 38 . . . R-Q8.

BLACK/FISCHER

WHITE/SPASSKY

40 . . . Q-B8ch

The adjourned game ended, as predicted by many analysts, in a perpetual check. Both players had decided overnight that there was no future in continuing the struggle. It was Spassky who was on the defensive, and he was glad to accept the draw offered by Fischer.

Fischer miscalculated in the early part of the game, allowing the champion to win a pawn. While he managed to regain the initiative, in the opinion of the experts, he, like Spassky, then lost his way in what should have been a winning continuation.

At the resumption of the game Schmid opened Spassky's sealed move. As everybody had expected, it was R-QN2. It took only three moves for Fischer and Spassky to decide on a draw.

WHITE/SPASSKY

Final Position

Following are the moves in the 15th game:

White Spassky	Black Fischer	White Spassky	Black Fischer
1 P-K4	P-QB4	23 P-K5	PxP
2 N-KB3	P-Q3	24 PxP	B-KR1
3 P-Q4	PxP	25 N-B3	R-Q1
4 NxP	N-KB3	26 RxRch	RxR
5 N-QB3	P-QR3	27 N-KN5	BxP
6 B-KN5	P-K3	28 QxP	R-Q2
7 P-B4	B-K2	29 QxRP	BxN
8 Q-B3	Q-B2	30 PxB	Q-N3ch
9 O-O-O	QN-Q2	31 K-B1	Q-R4
10 B-Q3	P-N4	32 Q-R8ch	K-R2
11 KR-K1	B-N2	33 P-QR4	N-Q6ch
12 Q-N3	O-O-O	34 BxN	RxB
13 BxN	NxB	35 K-B2	R-Q4
14 QxP	QR-B1	36 R-K4	R-Q1
15 Q-N3	P-N5	37 Q-N7	Q-KB4
16 N-R4	KR-N1	38 K-N3	Q-Q4ch
17 Q-B2	N-Q2	39 K-R3	Q-Q7
18 K-N1	K-N1	40 R-QN4	Q-B8ch
19 P-B3	N-B4	41 R-N2	Q-R8ch
20 B-B2	PxP	42 R-R2	Q-B8ch
21 NxBP	B-KB3	43 R-QN2	Q-R8ch
22 P-KN3	P-KR4	Drawn	

SCORE: Spassky 6 Fischer 9

Game Sixteen

The 16th game was devoid of excitement. Judging from the choice of the opening moves, both players seemed content to play for a draw.

After 34 moves, Spassky had a rook and two connected pawns, and Fischer had a rook and a pawn. The ending at that point was a theoretical draw, but, amazingly enough, play continued through 60 moves before the players agreed to a draw.

Before the start of the game, the world champion should have, and probably had, made an assessment of his chances in the remaining nine games, in which he would have the white pieces four times and the black pieces five. He must have pondered over what would be the correct plan for the nine games, in which he had to overcome a deficit of 3 points.

In deciding what course to pursue, he must have been haunted by his poor performance in the last three games, in which he only won 1 point, but should have scored 2½ and thus tied the match—an extremely disturbing and discouraging thought.

Spassky had to decide whether he should play safely with the Black pieces, content with splitting the points, and play for victories with the White pieces, or go all out with the Black pieces as well.

Fischer opened with P-K4 and Spassky did likewise, avoiding the Sicilian Defense. Spassky's choice of the opening indicated clearly that he had decided to play conservatively with Black, at least, in this game.

Fischer played the Ruy Lopez, which was expected, but on his fourth turn, he took Black's knight, instead of retreating the bishop to QR4. The line selected by Fischer was simplifying and tends to lead to even positions, offering little play for either side.

Fischer, with the commanding lead he enjoyed, was apparently reluctant to undertake aggressive action where risk might be involved, and was satisfied instead with splitting the point.

Black's 10 . . . N-B3 was new. Usual was 10 . . . P-QN4, preventing White's queen knight from reaching QB4, attacking Black's king bishop and king pawn.

After 11 moves, the champion was saddled with the double queen bishop pawns, which is usually a disadvantage, but he had, as compensation, two bishops against Fischer's knight and bishop.

Move 13 . . . B-KB4 would be imprudent because of 14 P-KN4, B-K3; 15 R-K3 threatening to win the queen bishop pawn after the knight moved. Consequently, Spassky decided the best move was to give up his queen bishop for Fischer's knight.

Black's provocative 14 . . . P-QN4 was an attempt to initiate action on the queen wing, but it involved the danger of weakening Black's pawn structure.

Fischer reacted with 15 P-B4, offering a pawn. If 15 . . . PxP; 16 R-Q4, regaining the pawn, and Black's pawn position would be wrecked.

Fischer's 15th move turned out to be premature. The champion's 15 . . . QR-N1 was an excellent strategical try, enabling him to open the queen knight file for action.

In order not to undouble Spassky's pawns, Fischer gave up a pawn, and this saddled Spassky with triple queen bishop pawns.

BLACK/SPASSKY

WHITE/FISCHER

19 . . . R-K5

Spassky attempted to capitalize on his extra pawn but Fischer's stubborn and accurate defense thwarted the champion's effort to make any appreciable headway.

BLACK/SPASSKY

WHITE/FISCHER

Final Position

Following are the moves of the 16th game:

White Fischer	Black Spassky	White Fischer	Black Spassky
1 P-K4	P-K4	21 R/1-B2	K-B2
2 N-KB3	N-QB3	22 K-N2	RxP
3 B-N5	P-QR3	23 K-B3	P-B6
4 BxN	QPxB	24 KxR	PxR
5 O-O	P-B3	25 RxQP	R-N4
6 P-Q4	B-KN5	26 R-B2	B-Q3
7 PxP	QxQ	27 RxP	R-QR4
8 RxQ	PxP	28 B-B4	R-R5ch
9 R-Q3	B-Q3	29 K-B3	R-R6ch
10 N/1-Q2	N-B3	30 K-K4	RxRP
11 N-B4	NxP	31 BxB	PxB
12 N/4xP	B/5xN	32 RxQP	RxP
13 NxB	O-O	33 RxP	RxP
14 B-K3	P-QN4	34 K-B3	R-Q7
15 P-B4	QR-N1	35 R-R7ch	K-B3
16 R-QB1	PxP	36 R-R6ch	K-K2
17 R-Q4	KR-K1	37 R-R7ch	R-Q2
18 N-Q2	NxN	38 R-R2	K-K3
19 RxN	R-K5	39 K-N2	R-K2
20 P-KN3	B-K4	40 K-R3	K-B3

White Fischer	Black Spassky	White Fischer	Black Spassky
41 R-R6ch	R-K3	52 K-R4	R-K5ch
42 R-R5	P-KR3	53 K-R3	R-K2
43 R-R2	K-B4	54 K-R4	R-K4
44 R-B2ch	K-N4	55 R-N6	K-N2
45 R-B7	P-N3	56 R-N4	K-R3
46 R-B4	P-R4	57 R-N6	R-K8
47 R-B3	R-KB3	58 K-R3	R-R8ch
48 R-R3	R-K3	59 K-N2	R-R8
49 R-KB3	R-K5	60 K-R3	R-R5
50 R-R3	K-R3	Drawn	
51 R-R6	R-K4		

SCORE: Spassky 6½ Fischer 9½

Game Seventeen

Spassky, conducting the white pieces, made a strong bid for a victory in the 17th game.

Spassky sacrificed a pawn early in the game for attacking prospects but, to curb White's assault, Fischer gave up his rook for a bishop.

Before the start of the game, Spassky was faced with a real dilemma. Coming down the stretch with only eight games remaining in which to overcome a handicap of 3 points, the Russian had to win this game—he had to throw all caution to the wind. This course involved the risk of defeat, which he could ill afford.

Spassky opened with P-K4. The king-pawn opening leads more to attacking and combinative possibilities than the queen-pawn opening, which develops into positional strategy. Spassky's forte is the former; the champion's shift to the queen-pawn opening is a recent development.

The American challenger's reply was 1 . . . P-Q3. If memory serves, he had never resorted to this move in serious competition. A familiar line of the Pirc Defense resulted.

If 7 PxP, NxP, Black would regain his pawn with

excellent play. White's next three moves were part of his natural development, enabling him to castle.

After nine moves White had a slight theoretical advantage. To increase this to something more substantial required hard work in an effort to introduce strategical and tactical ideas of a substantive nature.

Two ideas worthy of consideration were 10 P-QR3, to be followed by P-QN4, driving away the queen. Or 10 Q-K1, with the threat of N-Q5, threatening to win the king pawn, and if 10 . . . N-B3, 11 N-Q2, threatening to trap Black's queen bishop with P-B5.

Spassky's 12 B-B4 was significant, as it posted this bishop on a more favorable square. It also had a strong defensive idea, directed against Fischer's reply of 12 . . . N-Q2, exerting pressure against White's queen knight with his bishop and queen. Spassky would then parry this threat with 13 R-Q5, and if 13 . . . Q-N5, 14 R-N5, trapping the queen.

On his 13th turn, Spassky could have played safely by playing 13 Q-K1, protecting his queen knight, but he preferred to sacrifice a pawn. Fischer accepted and Spassky obtained attacking chances.

The question was, would Fischer be able to defend successfully? The complex position was full of possibilities, but only lengthy analysis could have given a definite answer.

A stronger alternative was 17 . . . Q-N5, attacking the king pawn, and after White protected the pawn, Fischer could continue with . . . N-K4, where the knight would be favorably posted for defense.

Fischer's 21 . . . Q-K4 gave his opponent the exchange. The challenger rejected 21 . . . KR-B1, fearing 22 B-N5, attacking the knight and eventually regaining his pawn, with the better ending.

The obvious 25 . . . R-B8 would fail because of 26 R/3-B3, and Black would win the king pawn, but White would gain control of the queen bishop file after the exchange of rooks.

Fischer's 33 . . . R-KB8 was to keep White's king off White's KB2, after which Spassky could force the exchange of rooks with R-K1. More productive would be 35 R-B4, followed by K-B2.

BLACK/FISCHER

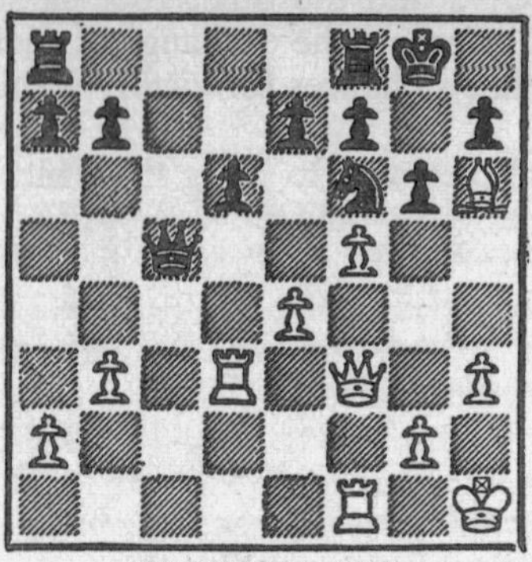

WHITE/SPASSKY

21 K-R1

After five moves were played in the adjourned position Fischer and Spassky agreed to a draw by repetition of moves. Spassky could have tried for a victory, but he and his aides apparently felt the chance of victory was too small to warrant the risk of losing.

The adjourned position was more intricate than it first appeared. Spassky, who played the white pieces, held a material advantage, consisting of two rooks and five pawns against Fischer's rook, knight and six pawns.

This plus would ordinarily suffice for a victory, but Spassky was concerned about his weak, isolated king pawn. In addition, Fischer's rook was favorably placed on the eighth rank, tying down one of Spassky's rooks.

Spassky's sealed move 41 R/KB2-QB2 was not the best. Better would be P-KR4, with the possibility of establishing a passed king rook pawn at the opportune moment by following it with P-KN4. Fischer's reply 41 . . . P-KN4 precluded that.

At adjournment there were four plans available to Spassky. The first was to attempt to obtain a passed king rook pawn. This would take a long time. Fischer could probably impede the pawn's advance by coordinated action of his king, rook and knight.

The second plan was to place the white king at KB2,

one rook at QN2 and the other rook at K2, with the threat of R-K1, forcing the exchange of rooks. Had this been done, White's chances for victory would have been promising.

The third plan was to bring the white king to the queen side, where it would be in a position to assist in the advance of White's queen side pawns. In the last two cases Fischer's counterplay would have been to bring his king to the center (K4) and exert pressure against White's king pawn.

The fourth plan was to play 41 R-QN2, in an attempt to advance the queen knight pawn. If Black decided to prevent this advance by continuing 41 . . . P-R4, then White would enhance his chances by playing 42 R-Q2, K-B3; 43 R-Q5, RxP; 44 R-QN5, regaining the pawn and penetrating Black's position. After Black would be compelled to move his knight, White would make further progress with R-QR4.

Spassky must have considered these ideas thoroughly. His immediate repetition of moves after adjournment was a strong indication that he had little faith in the success of these plans. He therefore probably decided to take the draw, theoretically, at least, leaving him with a chance to win the match.

BLACK/FISCHER

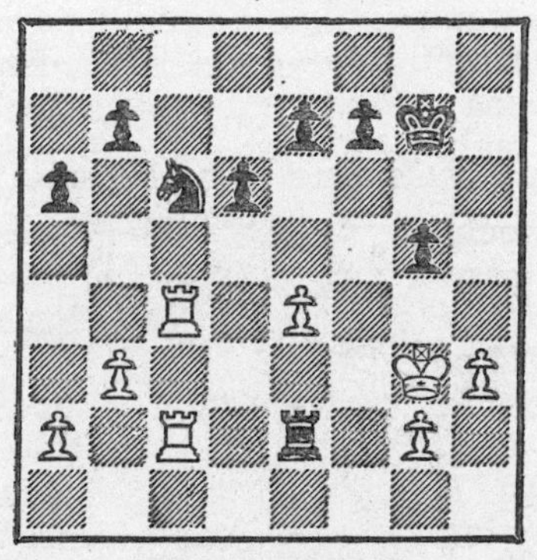

WHITE/SPASSKY

Final Position

Following are the moves of the 17th game:

White Spassky	Black Fischer	White Spassky	Black Fischer
1 P-K4	P-Q3	24 PxP	RPxP
2 P-Q4	P-KN3	25 Q-B4	QxQ
3 N-QB3	N-KB3	26 RxQ	N-Q2
4 P-B4	B-N2	27 R-B2	N-K4
5 N-B3	P-B4	28 K-R2	R-B8
6 PxP	Q-R4	29 R/3-K2	N-B3
7 B-Q3	QxBP	30 R-B2	R-K8
8 Q-K2	O-O	31 KR-K2	R-QR8
9 B-K3	Q-QR4	32 K-N3	K-N2
10 O-O	B-N5	33 QR-Q2	R-KB8
11 QR-Q1	N-B3	34 R-KB2	R-K8
12 B-B4	N-R4	35 KR-K2	R-KB8
13 B-N3	BxQN	36 R-K3	P-QR3
14 PxB	QxBP	37 R-QB3	R-K8
15 P-B5	N-B3	38 R-B4	R-KB8
16 P-KR3	BxN	39 R/2-QB2	R-QR8
17 QxB	N-QR4	40 R-B2	R-K8
18 R-Q3	Q-B2	41 R/2-B2	P-KN4
19 B-R6	NxB	42 R-B1	R-K7
20 BPxN	Q-B4ch	43 R/1-B2	R-K8
21 K-R1	Q-K4	44 R-B1	R-K7
22 BxR	RxB	45 R/1-B2	
23 R-K3	R-B1	Drawn	

SCORE: Spassky 7 Fischer 10

Game Eighteen

The 18th game of the match was a fierce battle. Spassky, playing the black pieces, concentrated on attacking, but later changed his mind and shifted to positional strategy. He made a few questionable moves, exposing his king dangerously, but precise play kept him alive.

Spassky tried valiantly to get back into the running, but Fischer's stubborn resistance stopped him cold. Fischer, playing the white pieces, returned to the king pawn opening. Spassky replied 1 . . . P-QB4, relying on the Sicilian Defense, which he had not resorted to since the third game. The reason for his choice of opening was that the Sicilian Defense offers Black better winning chances than any other opening. The world champion thus indicated clearly that he was looking for a fight.

Fischer's eighth move, castling on the queen wing, was acceptance of Spassky's challenge for a battle.

Spassky advanced his queenside pawns in preparation for an assault on White's king.

White's 17 R-QB1 was a preparatory move. It was directed toward a possible opening of the queen bishop line with P-B3. That would be plausible if the champion continued to press his attack with . . . P-R6. Fischer would then continue P-QN3, and the queen rook file would be closed, reducing Black's attacking prospects, after which White would be in a position to play P-B3.

Spassky's 18 . . . P-N6, closing up the queen knight file, thereby abandoned a direct attack against White's king. This was a dubious decision. He shifted to a positional type of game. The explanation for his decision is that if he continued 18 . . . PxP; 19 RxP, Q-N3; 20 B-B4, exerting annoying pressure against Black's king pawn.

Spassky's 18th move, however, reduced his chances of a victory. It would, therefore, have been more prudent to have continued with 18 . . . N-K4, preventing White from placing his bishop on Q-B4, and, at the same time, keeping the queen knight file open.

Preferable was 20 PxP, PxP; 21 N-Q4 or 20 N-Q4, exerting pressure on Black's king pawn.

Fischer's 22 QR-K1 offered Spassky a pawn. If he had taken it, Fischer would have had a powerful attack because of the open king file.

Black's 22 . . . K-Q1 was to get the king out of danger, since White had his pieces lined up for aggressive action. With the black king on K1, White was in a position to sacrifice his knight at his Q5 at the opportune moment. Consequently, Black's king was placed on a safer square.

The tempting, freeing 25 . . . P-K4 would fail on account of 26 N-B3, P-Q4; 27 N(Q3)xP with a clearly won position.

Note that after 29 NxR, QPxN; 30 N-B3, B-B3, Black would have more than sufficient compensation for the exchange. His bishops would become extremely active.

The move 34 . . . RxP would fail against 35 N-B4, which would win the exchange.

Too risky was 31 . . . P-K4. The move 34 . . . QxQP was an error. Correct was 34 . . . R-Q1; 35 N-B4, QxQ; 36 RxQ, K-Q3, with a complicated position.

The adjourned position of the game was complex, with numerous variations and subvariations. Fischer, Spassky and their seconds must have spent a sleepless night in exhaustive analysis.

BLACK/SPASSKY

WHITE/FISCHER

42 Q-K6

Each player had a problem in the adjourned position. White's king position in the corner subjected it to a possible mating net, if Black's queen or rook were permitted to reach White's first rank. Consequently, a White rook had to be placed at QN1, immobilizing it temporarily.

Black's problem was its exposed king, subject to harassment by White's queen and other rook. It was mandatory for Black to prevent R-QN7ch, which could have led to mate.

Spassky's sealed move 42 . . . Q-B3 was best. The move 42 . . . Q-K3 would lose to 43 Q-N7 with the imminent threat of 44 Q-R7ch or Q-N7 mate. Possible would have been 42 . . . Q-Q3, and if White persisted with 43 Q-N7, threatening mate, Black could have parried the threat with 43 . . . R-B2.

If now White had exchanged rooks and queens and advanced his king rook pawn, Black's king could have been brought over to the kingside in time to stop the pawn. Black's position would have been satisfactory.

Black's 44 . . . Q-KB6 was imperative. It prevented 45 Q-K3ch, R-Q5; 46 Q-B2, in which case Black could not have protected his bishop pawn.

A relevant question is, why did Fischer not try for a win by trying to promote his king rook pawn on his 44th turn by playing P-KR4? What could Spassky have done to counteract this plan? He could have played 44 . . . Q-B7; 45 P-R5 (45 RxP? QxQ, winning a rook) QxQ; 46 PxQ, R-KN1, and the result would have been a double-edged position.

BLACK/SPASSKY

WHITE/FISCHER

Final Position

Following are the moves of the 18th game:

White Fischer	Black Spassky	White Fischer	Black Spassky
1 P-K4	P-QB4	5 NxP	N-B3
2 N-KB3	P-Q3	6 B-KN5	P-K3
3 N-QB3	N-QB3	7 Q-Q2	P-QR3
4 P-Q4	PxP	8 O-O-O	B-Q2

White Fischer	Black Spassky	White Fischer	Black Spassky
9 P-B4	B-K2	29 Q-K2	R-R4
10 N-B3	P-N4	30 PxP	PxP
11 BxN	PxB	31 R-B2	P-K4
12 B-Q3	Q-R4	32 N-KB5	BxN
13 K-N1	P-N5	33 RxB	P-Q4
14 N-K2	Q-QB4	34 PxP	QxQP
15 P-B5	P-QR4	35 N-N4	Q-Q2
16 N-B4	P-R5	36 RxRP	BxN
17 R-QB1	R-QN1	37 BPxB	R-Q4
18 P-B3	P-N6	38 R-B1ch	K-N2
19 P-QR3	N-K4	39 Q-K4	R-QB1
20 KR-B1	N-B5	40 R-QN1	K-N3
21 BxN	QxB	41 R-R7	R-Q5
22 QR-K1	K-Q1	42 Q-N6	Q-B3
23 K-R1	R-N4	43 R-KB7	R-Q3
24 N-Q4	R-R4	44 Q-KR6	Q-KB6
25 N-Q3	K-B2	45 Q-R7	Q-B3
26 N-N4	P-R4	46 Q-R6	Q-KB6
27 P-KN3	R-K4	47 Q-R7	Q-B3
28 N-Q3	R-QN1	Drawn	

SCORE: Spassky 7½ Fischer 10½

Game Nineteen

The 19th game of the match was exciting and nerve-racking for both players. Spassky attacked fiercely, but Fischer's cool and stubborn defense parried every threat successfully. After 26 moves, an even end-game was reached, and the players agreed on a draw after 40 moves.

Spassky, playing White, once again opened with P-K4. Fischer replied 1 . . . N-KB3, the second time that the Alekhine Defense, has been played in the match.

Spassky failed to obtain an appreciable opening advantage. He did acquire a bind on the center, but Fischer quickly struck at Spassky's pawn formation. After 17 moves, chances appeared even for both sides.

On his 18th turn, Spassky unexpectedly sacrificed a knight, and the fight was on. Fischer declined the gift.

Spassky made another surprising move on his 19th

turn, posing serious problems for his opponent. Fischer seemed to be in trouble. Spassky sacrificed another piece on his 20th move and threatened to expose Fischer's king to an irresistible attack.

WHITE/SPASSKY

19 . . . B-R5

Fischer defended accurately, and he was able to neutralize the position by giving up a rook and two pawns for a bishop and a knight. The resultant endgame was an easy draw.

On his 12th move, Spassky had to make a decision —whether to play 12 PxB, forcing Black to retreat his king knight to Q2. But in doing so, White would have weakened his king's position considerably. The continuation might have been: 12 PxB, KN-Q2; 13 P-B4; 14 PxP e.p., NxP; 15 B-Q3, with the idea of continuing P-B5, undoubling the king bishop pawns. Spassky elected to maintain a sound pawn structure.

On move 13, Spassky preferred giving up his bishop rather than playing 13 B-B1 and driving away the knight with 14 P-QN3, which would have given Spassky better prospects for an opening advantage than the move he played.

Another possibility for Black would have been 16 . . . P-QR4 in an attempt to liquidate the pawn situation on the queen side, and if Spassky would have continued 17 P-R3, Fischer could have opened the queen rook file with 17 . . . RPxP. Bad for White would have been, in this, 17 P-N5 because of 17 . . . NPxP; 18 NPxP, NxP, with promising play for Black.

After 18 NxP, White's knight was immune to capture. For if 18 . . . KPxN; 19 PxP, PxP; 20 BxP, N-Q2; 21 BxR, RxB; 22 RxP! and if 22 . . . KxR; 23 Q-B3ch, winning the rook, with a won position.

Fischer's reply to Spassky's 18th move was the only try at imprisoning the knight—but could it ever have been captured?

Spassky's 19 B-R5 was a fascinating try. It had a double threat: either 20 Q-N4 or 20 BxPch, RxB; 21 RxR, KxR; 22 Q-R5ch, with an irresistible assault.

After 19 . . . BPxN, 20 BxPch, the reply 20 . . . K-R1 would have been insufficient because of 21 PxP, N-R3; 22 BxP with four pawns for the piece and good winning chances.

Worthy of consideration was 21 . . . Q-Q1, and the onus would have been on Spassky to prove that his sacrifice of the bishop was sound. Fischer's 21 . . . Q-Q7 was for the purpose of forcing the exchange of queens, leading into an interesting and difficult end-game.

BLACK/FISCHER

WHITE/SPASSKY

Final Position

Spassky was unable to avoid the exchange of queens. If 22 Q-KB1, QxPch; 23 K-R1, N-B3 with the advantage.

Capture of the pawn by Black on his 27th turn would have cost a piece after White played 28 R-QB7.

Following are the moves of the 19th game:

White Spassky	Black Fischer	White Spassky	Black Fischer
1 P-K4	N-KB3	21 RxR	Q-Q7
2 P-K5	N-Q4	22 QxQ	BxQ
3 P-Q4	P-Q3	23 R/1-KB1	N-B3
4 N-KB3	B-N5	24 PxP	PxP
5 B-K2	P-K3	25 R-Q7	B-K6ch
6 O-O	B-K2	26 K-R1	BxP
7 P-KR3	B-R4	27 P-K6	B-K4
8 P-B4	N-N3	28 RxQP	R-K1
9 N-B3	O-O	29 R-K1	RxP
10 B-K3	P-Q4	30 R-Q6	K-B2
11 P-B5	BxN	31 RxN	RxR
12 BxB	N-B5	32 RxB	K-B3
13 P-QN3	NxB	33 R-Q5	K-K3
14 PxN	P-QN3	34 R-R5	P-R3
15 P-K4	P-QB3	35 K-R2	R-R3
16 P-QN4	NPxP	36 P-B6	RxBP
17 NPxP	Q-R4	37 R-R5	P-R3
18 NxP	B-N4	38 K-N3	K-B3
19 B-R5	BPxN	39 K-B3	R-B6ch
20 BxPch	RxB	40 K-K2	R-B7ch
		Drawn	

SCORE: Spassky 8 Fischer 11

Game Twenty

The opening and the middle game of the 20th game of the match were relatively insignificant, but an intense struggle developed in the end game.

Bobby Fischer, playing white, relied on the king pawn opening. Spassky once again responded with the Sicilian Defense.

On his 10th turn, Fischer varied from a previous game by continuing 10 B-K2, a relatively new move. Spassky then castled on the king side, presaging a hard struggle.

On his 12th move, Fischer decided to play safely and adopted a plan of simplification by forcing the exchange of queens and some minor pieces.

The ending reached appeared simple, with the outlook of a draw. But Spassky decided to complicate matters. He avoided the exchange of the remaining rooks, and an intense struggle followed.

Spassky pressed on, outplaying the challenger. Strategical and tactical maneuvers followed by both sides, in which Fischer seemed to flounder and Spassky to seize the initiative.

A good alternative to the text would have been 11 N-B3, intending 12 P-K5. If, for instance, 12 . . . Q-B2; 13 P-K5, and if Black continued 13 . . . PxP? 14 BxN would have won a piece. One possibility for Black would have been 11 . . . P-N4, and if 12 P-K5, P-N5, with great complications.

White's move 11 B-B3 was for the purpose of protecting the king pawn, thereby threatening to break up Black's king position: 12 NxN, BxN; 13 BxN, PxB (if 13 . . . BxB, White would have won a pawn with 14 QxP) and Black's king position would be insecure.

Black's 11 . . . P-R3 meant that if Fischer had played 12 BxN, Spassky would have been prepared to recapture the bishop with the pawn, instead of with the bishop. He could then have initiated an attack on the queen wing, and a real battle could have ensued.

Bad for Black would have been 14 . . . NxN on account of 15 BxP, QRxB; 16 RxN, attacking the knight and the queen rook pawn.

Simpler for Black would have been 16 . . . B-K1; 17 KR-Q1, RxR; 18 RxR, R-Q1, 19 RxR, NxR, and White's queen knight would not have been in a position to get to QR4. If White had then attempted to reach QB5 by playing 20 N-K4, Spassky could have met that intention by playing either 20 . . . P-QN3 or 20 . . . B-B3, in either case with a satisfactory position.

Spassky's 20 . . . R-N1 was a desperate try to

win. Unsatisfactory for him would have been 20 . . . RxRch; 21 KxR—the knight's pressure on queen side pawns would have forced Black to retreat his knight awkwardly to Q1, but the position would have been tenable.

Another possibility for White was 21 R-K1 with the intention of striking at Black's king pawn with P-KB5.

The move 21 . . . N-N5 would have failed against 22 R-N3, and if 22 . . . NxRPch; 23 K-N1, with the knight trapped.

If Black had played 22 . . . P-QN3, instead of 22 . . . P-QN4, Fischer could have forced a draw with 23 N-R6, R-N2; 24 N-B5, etc.

The move 28 . . . P-N5 would have been inadvisable because of 29 R-B4, PxP; 30 PxP, N-R4; 31 R-B7ch, K-Q3; 32 R-KR7, with Black's king pawns under fire.

White's 29 N-B5 was inferior. Better was 29 N-N4.

Faulty would have been 29 . . . B-N3 on account of 30 NxKP, P-N5; 31 R-K3, R-K1; 34 P-B5! BxP; 35 N-N7, winning a pawn.

The tempting but dubious 31 . . . B-N3 would have been met by 32 N-B2, attacking the knight and the king knight pawn simultaneously.

BLACK/SPASSKY

WHITE/FISCHER

41 N-Q1

With the resumption of the game Fischer was on the defensive.

Spassky tried desperately to lure Fischer into committing the slightest error and when Fischer refused to oblige, a draw was agreed upon after 54 moves. Spassky finally realized that he was unable to make any headway.

At adjournment, Fischer had two knights and five pawns against Spassky's bishop, knight and five pawns.

Spassky's pawn position was superior to that of Fischer; Spassky's pieces were more favorably posted than his opponent's. But Spassky's bishop controlled white squares while a majority of Fischer's pawns were on black squares so that the bishop could not have been utilized to harass the pawns.

Fischer was in no position to undertake anything. His pieces were posted favorably for defensive purposes only. His only weakness was a backward king rook pawn, which was threatened with attack by his opponent's knight.

Fischer solved his problem satisfactorily by placing his knight at K1, preventing the incursion of Spassky's knight.

Spassky's only dim hope for victory was to create a passed pawn and penetrate with his king into his opponent's territory. But this, even if achieved, would not have sufficed.

After Black's 46 . . . K-Q3, the threat was 47 . . . B-N3ch, which wins. Spassky was enticing Fischer to play for a victory with 47 N-B5ch.

This could have been followed by 47 . . . NxN; 48 KxN, K-Q4 with superior chances for Black, because Black would have been in a position to advance his king pawn and penetrate with his king. Fischer wisely rejected the temptation.

Spassky would have accomplished nothing with 48 . . . N-B6 (attempting to obtain a passed pawn) on account of 47 NxN, PxN; 48 K-Q2, K-B4; 49 P-B3, followed by K-KI-B2, and Black's king could never have crossed the fourth rank, with White marking time with his king.

The move 49 . . . BxN would have been futile,

BLACK/SPASSKY

WHITE/FISCHER

Final Position

for it could have been followed by 50 KxB, N-B6; 51 N-B1, P-N5 (the only try; if 51 . . . K-Q4, N-K3ch, preventing the advance of the king pawn, and, after the king moves, N-B1 again) 52 PxPch, KxP; 53 K-K4, and Black could not have made any progress.

The following are the moves in the 20th game:

White Fischer	Black Spassky	White Fischer	Black Spassky
1 P-K4	P-QB4	19 RxR	RxR
2 N-KB3	N-QB3	20 N-B5	R-N1
3 P-Q4	PxP	21 R-Q3	P-QR4
4 NxP	N-B3	22 R-N3	P-QN4
5 N-QB3	P-Q3	23 P-QR3	P-R5
6 B-KN5	P-K3	24 R-B3	R-Q1
7 Q-Q2	P-QR3	25 N-Q3	P-B3
8 O-O-O	B-Q2	26 R-B5	R-N1
9 P-B4	B-K2	27 R-B3	P-N4
10 B-K2	O-O	28 P-KN3	K-Q3
11 B-B3	P-R3	29 N-B5	P-KN5
12 B-R4	NxP	30 N-K4ch	K-K2
13 BxB	NxQ	31 N-K1	R-Q1
14 BxQ	NxB	32 N-Q3	R-Q5
15 NxN/3	KRxB	33 N/4-B2	P-R4
16 RxP	K-B1	34 R-B5	R-Q4
17 KR-Q1	K-K2	35 R-B3	N-Q5
18 N-QR4	B-K1	36 R-B7ch	R-Q2

White Fischer	Black Spassky	White Fischer	Black Spassky
37 RxRch	BxR	47 K-Q3	B-N3ch
38 N-K1	P-K4	48 K-B3	K-B4
39 PxP	PxP	49 N-Q3ch	K-Q3
40 K-Q2	B-B4	50 N-K1	K-B3
41 N-Q1	K-Q3	51 K-Q2	K-B4
42 N-K3	B-K3	52 N-Q3ch	K-Q3
43 K-Q3	B-B2	53 N-K1	N-K3
44 K-B3	K-B3	54 K-B3	N-Q5
45 K-Q3	K-B4	Drawn	
46 K-K4	K-Q3		

SCORE: Spassky 8½ Fischer 11½

Game Twenty-One

The 21st game was interesting and absorbing. Spassky played enterprisingly, sacrificing the exchange and obtaining a good position. But he later mishandled the end game and, at adjournment, Fischer stood better.

Spassky opened with the king pawn. Fischer, although having had two successes in the match with the Alekhine Defense, returned to the Sicilian Defense in an obvious effort to get his opponent off balance.

On his seventh move, Fischer veered away from the trodden path, as is his custom, and made an unusual move. The opening then changed in nature. It turned into a Scotch Opening variation, with the slight difference that White's queen bishop was developed at Q4, instead of KN5.

Spassky embarked on a plan of exchanging queens to weaken Black's pawn structure on the king wing. As compensation, Fischer had the two bishops.

On his 18th turn, Fischer made a dubious move. Spassky immediately sacrificed the exchange, obtaining a bishop and a pawn for a rook. He appeared to have winning chances because of his two passed pawns on the queen's wing, but Fischer found an adequate defense to hold the position. Spassky, pressing too hard for a victory, went astray and handed the initiative to his opponent.

The move 12 . . . B-KN5 would have been a blunder because of 13 BxN, BxQ; 14 QRxB, putting White a piece ahead.

An interesting move, which was discarded by Fischer, was 12 . . . N-N5, which could have been followed by 13 P-KR3, Q-R5 (if 13 . . . N-R7; 14 Q-R5, P-N3; 15 Q-R6 with advantage) 14 KR-K1, N-R7, with complications.

The move 13 B-K5 was worthy of consideration, and the reply 13 . . . BxB could have been met by 14 RxB, with advantage for White because of Black's inferior pawn structure.

After White's 16 QR-Q1, the threat was 17 B-B4. Another move Fischer had to contend with was 17 B-K4.

Fischer's reply 16 . . . KR-K1 met the aforementioned threats.

The move 18 NxP would have been a blunder on account of 18 . . . BxN; 19 RxB, BxPch, winning the exchange.

The preferable move was 20 . . . PxP, which could have been followed by 21 BPxP (if 21 RPxP, a similar position to the actual play would have arisen, with the important difference that Black's king would have been nearer the passed pawns, being in a position to stop their advance more readily) BxPch; 22 KxB, RxR; 23 BxP, R-R1! and if 24 B-N7, R-R4ch, followed by . . . RxP.

It would have been hopeless for Fischer to play 27 . . . RxP, for it could have led to 28 P-R5, R-R7; 29 P-R6, followed by the immediate advance of the queen knight pawn, and the black king would not have been in time to stop this pawn's advance. Black's 27 . . . R-R7 was the only possible course to stop the immediate advance of White's queen rook pawn.

A wiser course for White would have been 29, P-B4, followed by keeping the king at KN3 and KR3, and Black could not have made any progress.

Spassky resigned the game without resuming play.

The adjourned position—which became, of course,

the final position—was extremely interesting. Spassky, white, had a bishop and four pawns, while Fischer had a rook and two pawns. Spassky, however, had two passed pawns on the queen side. Fischer's rook was behind these pawns, preventing their advance, which, if permitted, could have become dangerous.

Fischer's only chance of victory consisted of posting his king at KN5 and advancing his king rook pawn to KR6, driving White's king to his first rank, after which Black could have checked at QR8. White's king could have gone to KR2, and Fischer's rook could have moved to KB8. White's king bishop pawn would have been lost. Then Fischer could have advanced his king to KN6, and the threat of . . . P-R7 and . . . R-KB8 mate could not have been parried.

Spassky could have put up resistance in the adjourned position. Had Fischer had his king at KN5 or his king rook pawn at KR5, Spassky could have placed his bishop on the diagonal KR1-QR8, to meet the threat of P-R6ch with B-B3ch, driving away the black king.

It is true that Black would have won White's king bishop pawn in this variation, but that would have been unimportant to the defense set up by Spassky. His bishop could then have gone to QB6, threatening to

WHITE/SPASSKY

BLACK/FISCHER

Final Position

advance his queen knight pawn. Had Fischer permitted this, the challenger's winning chances would not have been bright.

In any case, the win for Fischer was not clear. Spassky probably decided against continuing in the adjourned position because he thought it not worth the effort. Even if he had drawn this game, his chances of recovery in the match would have been practically nil.

Following are the moves of the 21st game:

White Spassky	Black Fischer	White Spassky	Black Fischer
1 P-K4	P-QB4	22 BxP	R-Q7
2 N-KB3	P-K3	23 BxRP	RxQBP
3 P-Q4	PxP	24 R-K2	RxR
4 NxP	P-QR3	25 BxR	R-Q1
5 N-QB3	N-QB3	26 P-R4	R-Q7
6 B-K3	N-KB3	27 B-B4	R-R7
7 B-Q3	P-Q4	28 K-N3	K-B1
8 PxP	PxP	29 K-B3	K-K2
9 O-O	B-Q3	30 P-KN4	P-B4
10 NxN	PxN	31 PxP	P-B3
11 B-Q4	O-O	32 B-N8	P-R3
12 Q-B3	B-K3	33 K-N3	K-Q3
13 KR-K1	P-B4	34 K-B3	R-R8
14 BxN	QxB	35 K-N2	K-K4
15 QxQ	PxQ	36 B-K6	K-B5
16 QR-Q1	KR-Q1	37 B-Q7	R-QN8
17 B-K2	QR-N1	38 B-K6	R-N7
18 P-QN3	P-B5	39 B-B4	R-R7
19 NxP	BxN	40 B-K6	P-R4
20 RxB	BxPch	Resigns	
21 KxB	RxR		

SCORE: Fischer 12½ Spassky 8½

PART THREE/Conclusion

6 The Wind-up

The chess match of the century ended with faint echoes of the way it had begun, with some confusion, some misunderstanding, with Fischer's temperamental, almost —some say—boorish behavior and with Spassky, the nice guy, finishing last.

The 21st game was a hard-fought one. Spassky, playing White, gave up the exchange on his 19th move, breaking up Fischer's pawn center and emerging with two dangerous passed pawns on the queen's wing. Fischer, by bringing his rook behind Spassky's pawns, managed to prevent them from moving. But his rook was immobilized, glued to its observation post.

A draw seemed to be coming up.

But Fischer doggedly pressed on and Spassky—as he had done so discouragingly many times in the match—misplayed, failing to find the best moves.

At adjournment, Fischer stood better, and one Belgian expert said to an American journalist after Spassky sealed his 41st move: "I congratulate you on your American world champion."

As WNET-TV, N.Y. (Channel 13) began its coverage of the match on the morning of Friday, September 1, word came over the wire agencies: Spassky had resigned.

The group of experts and commentators in the studio, together with Shelby Lyman, began a victory celebration.

A few minutes later the news agencies sent out a bulletin: the resignation story had been premature. Don't use it.

There was animated discussion in the studio—closely attended by the television audience—and then the analysis resumed. If Spassky played this, Fischer could reply with this, and if Spassky continued with this, Fischer could . . . and so on.

The analysts had just reached the conclusion that

Spassky could, after all, continue with a viable game, and might even be able to press his advantage, when the definitive word came.

Spassky had, indeed, resigned. He had done so by telephone (and thus the confusion, because the unsealed move was not "resigns"). The lights flashed on in the studio—"Spassky Resigns"—and the group resumed its victory party.

In Reykjavik, Lothar Schmid, after conferring with FIDE officials, walked to the front of the stage and addressed the audience, which had jammed the playing hall.

"Ladies and gentlemen," he said, "Mr. Spassky has resigned by telephone at 12:50."

The audience broke into applause. Fischer, busy signing his score sheet, nodded thanks.

"This is a traditional and legal way of resignation," Schmid continued. "Mr. Fischer has won this game number twenty-one, and he is the winner of the match."

Rhythmic hand-clapping swept through the audience, and those who had been sitting rose to their feet. There were shouts of "Bravo!" Fischer, still busying himself at the chessboard, again nodded, looked uncomfortable, glanced at the audience out of the corner of his eyes, and rushed off.

"What a way for it to end," an American said with a pained look. He and his friends had arrived at the playing hall three hours early to get a good seat for the finale.

Spassky apparently had made up his mind, after a night of analysis, that his position, his game, the match and the championship were lost. Soon after he had made this decision he ran into Harry Benson, a *Time-Life* photographer, at the Saga Hotel.

"There's a new champion," Spassky said to Benson. "I'm not sad. It's a sporting event and I lost. Bobby's the new champion. Now I must take a walk and get some fresh air."

Benson phoned Fischer with the news.

"You're sure it's official?" Fischer asked. "Well, thanks."

The ceremony was still to come, the counterpart of

the opening ceremony. But this time Fischer would be there, to accept the title, the applause, the glory, the money. It was scheduled for Sunday, in Exhibition Hall, and there was to be a Viking-style feast, dancing, speeches.

The final score: 12½ for the American challenger —7 victories, 11 draws, 3 losses (including the forfeit)—and 8½ for the now former champion—3 victories (including the forfeit), 11 draws, 7 losses.

The chess match of the century had ended.

7 The Transformed Future of Chess?—

Now that the chess match of the century is over; now that the championship has, for the first time since 1948, been wrested from the Russians; now that the city of Reykjavik has returned to normal and the chess-watchers have gone from the bizarre lava fields and craters and hot springs of Iceland; now that other sports—the kind where shouts, not silence, are the indices of spectators' passions—once more dominate TV and newspaper coverage; now that Bobby Fischer has returned triumphant with the world chess crown and an invitation to the White House (the first such ever extended to a chess champion) among his baggage . . .

Now what?

Will the chess world go back to what it was? Will tournaments, matches, olympiads, go back to the dim world of semi-oblivion they had long enjoyed—or endured? Will chess stars once again earn $500 plus expenses (if they are lucky) for winning a major event?

And will Bobby Fischer sink back into the public subconscious?

Grandmasters say no. The chess world, they say, can never be the same again. For Fischer has transformed it.

They discussed it in the press rooms, the cafeterias, the halls of Laugardalshöll during the match. No, they said, they would not be likely to play again for the pittances they used to get. Fischer, despite his antics, his tantrums, his sometimes silly, sometimes outlandish demands—Fischer has given them a dignity and a status they had never enjoyed before on so wide a scale.

Fischer, the upstart, the braggart, the uncivil, had earned for them and for their profession something that all the gentlemanly, decorous and even brilliant masters and grandmasters had never been able to earn: the respect of the public and the recognition that chess players, like golf pros and football heroes, are entitled to decent compensation for their time and talent.

During the match department stores in New York were selling chess sets as fast as they were promoting them. And they were promoting them—with full-page newspaper ads—as they never had before.

Crowds gathered on the streets of Manhattan to watch television coverage of the match. And when, one day, Channel 13 interrupted its chess coverage to switch to the Democratic national convention, it was swamped with complaints. It went back to chess after an hour.

The United States Chess Federation reported a tremendous spurt in membership applications.

Chess had arrived.

And what about the man who wrought this revolution? What about Fischer?

Before the match, Fischer was to chess what Joe Namath was to football—and then some. His international rating of about 2,800 points made him the highest-rated player in the history of the game, or at least the history of it since ratings were instituted.

And what did he earn from this exalted position? A million a year? Half a million? Two hundred thousand, perhaps?

Nothing near that.

"I've never needed much money," Fischer had said in an interview in 1971. "I've made a living at chess, but not a good living."

Fischer was one of perhaps half a dozen professional chess players in the United States and his pre-match income was perhaps $20,000 a year. He collected, for example, $7,500 as the winner's share of a $10,000 purse when he defeated Petrosian in Buenos Aires. That was high by chess-pro standards.

Asked in that same interview what he wanted from life, Fischer said:

"The world's championship. Recognition."

Now he has both. What will he do with them?

"When I win the championship," Fischer has said, "I won't wait three years to put it on the line. I'll play once, maybe twice, a year."

But will he be able to put his championship on the line?

Under FIDE rules, the championship match must be the culmination of the three-year cycle of regionals, interzonals and candidates' matches. There is no short cut. Thus, even if Fischer offers to put his title up in a match, it would be unofficial.

The champion could, however, ask FIDE to waive the rules, or to make special rules, or to set up a special title match. And if FIDE were to grant the request Fischer could, indeed, play "once, maybe twice, a year" for the title.

There is nothing to stop Fischer from playing a non-title match, of course (though anyone who beat him, even in a non-title match would undoubtedly proclaim himself the world champion—just as Fischer did for years). And, toward the end of the match in Reykjavik, rumors were flying that a Fischer-Spassky return match, with a million-dollar purse, was already being arranged for in Las Vegas.

Fischer was not the only chess star for whom a new world of glory, recognition and remuneration was opening. Offers—from TV shows, book and magazine publishers, chess-set manufacturers and countless other promoters were pouring in on people who, for years, had had to settle for a starvation living—or find their bread-money by teaching or driving cabs or doing something other than chess.

And all because of Bobby Fischer.

During the harrowing pre-match negotiations and disputes it was frequently said that Fischer never again would be invited to participate in a tournament or match; that no one would want to risk the investment knowing that Fischer might balk, refuse, back out or simply not show up.

But now that Fischer has displayed his brilliance, now that he has demonstrated that he is, indeed, the best in the world, now that those who decried his behavior have forgiven it, he is once again good box office and a prime piece of property.

But he is also the world champion of chess and

he is not likely to sell himself as simply just another property.

Chess has taken on new recognition and new dignity, and chess players will be taking advantage of their newfound leverage. And the best of them all, Bobby Fischer, will be in the best position of all to take advantage.

One thing is certain: Three years from now there will be a new match for the chess championship of the world.

Appendices

Appendix A

The following are the formal rules of the Fédération Internationale des Échecs for the competition for the world chess championships. Those provisions dealing only with the world women's championships have been deleted.

Art. 1

Introduction

The individual championships for men and ladies are to be contested according to a periodical system as set out in Art. 2 and 3.

Art. 2

Competition system for the Men's World Championship

a In the first year of the period Zonal Tournaments are to be organized in the zones of FIDE.
b in the second year, an Interzonal Tournament is to be organized;
c in the third year, a Candidates Competition is to be organized;
d in the fourth year, a match for the World Championship is to be organized.
The composition of each of the competitions as per b), c), and d) is based—entirely or partially—on the results of the competition immediately preceding.
In the same year as the match is organized for the World Championship, the zonal tournaments of the next period are to be organized, after which the subsequent competitions for that period follow in the order set out above.

Art. 4

Division into Zones. Special and General Rules

At the FIDE Congress of the year preceding that in which zonal tournaments are to be held, the division into zones for the next three-year period will be decided. At the same time the *special* rules applicable to the zonal and interzonal tournaments of the next period will be established, taking into account the strength of players in each zone and in the federations concerned.

The *special* rules set out in Art. 5–8 below will be applicable to the Candidates Competitions and to the matches for the World Championship.

The *general* rules set out in Art. 9–12 will be applicable to all competitions.

Art. 5

Men's Candidates Competition

1 The Men's Candidates Competition will take place once every three years with 8 participants, to wit:

   a the two players who obtained the two first places at the preceding Candidates Competition; if one of these players or both are unable to participate, they will be replaced by players in the same competition according to the list of results.

   However, if between the two Candidates Competitions the World Champion loses his title, the first of these two places will be his by right. Similarly, if in the same period a player plays a drawn title match with the World Champion, the same right will be accorded to him;

   b the six players who obtained the six first places at the preceding Interzonal Tournament; if one or several of these players are unable to participate, they will be replaced by other players in the same tournament in accordance with the list of results.

2 If a player authorized to participate in accordance with clause 1 a) is likewise authorized to participate in accordance with clause 1 b), then his participation will be considered to derive from the qualification in accordance with clause 1 a).

3 The Competition will be arranged in the form of matches between pairs of players, to wit:

   a four matches (quarterfinals) between the eight players authorized to participate;

   b two matches (semifinals) between the four winners of the quarter finals;

   c one match (final) between the two winners of the semifinals.

   Furthermore, a match will be organized

   d between the two losing players from the semifinals, this match to decide on the 3rd and the 4th placing at the competition.

4 After the termination of the interzonal tournament a list will be drawn up in which the eight players authorized to participate at the candidates competition are numbered from 1 to 8. The two players authorized to participate in virtue of clause 1 a) will be given the numbers 1 and 2. The order between them is determined, if both come from the preceding candidates competition, by their placing

there; if one is authorized to participate in accordance with the second section of clause 1 a), he will be given the number 1. The numbers 3 to 8 are given to the players from the interzonal tournament according to their placing in the tournament; if several players who may come into question here have obtained the same number of points, the order between them will be determined, if they are all qualified for participation, by drawing of lots, and in other cases by the procedure indicated in Article 12.2 C) below. The matches in the quarterfinals will be organized in such a way that according to a drawing of lots each of the players numbered 1 to 4 will have to meet one of the four players numbered 5 to 8. The drawing of lots is to be carried out as soon as possible by the President or a person nominated by him.

Immediately after the said drawing of lots, the President or his nominee will carry out a second drawing of lots to determine the pairing of the winners of the quarterfinals in the semifinals.

5 Each of the matches in the quarterfinals and semifinals will comprise 10 games, and the final match will comprise 12 games, while the special match for decision of the 3rd and 4th places will comprise 6 games; however, this last number may be increased to 8 or 10 by the President at the request of both players. If in a match in the quarterfinals, semifinals or finals the two players obtain the same number of points, a fresh drawing of lots will be undertaken concerning colours, and play will be continued until the first game won, though with the limitation that the decision will be arrived at by a drawing of lots if there have been a number of supplementary drawn games amounting, in a match in the quarterfinals and the match for the 3rd and 4th places to 4, in a match in the semifinals to 6 and in the final match to 8.

For all matches it is to be observed that if a player has obtained a result assuring him of the victory, the play will not be continued except by the common consent of the players.

6 The matches in the quarterfinals will, if possible, be arranged simultaneously and at the same place and will be followed, after a week of rest, by the semifinals. In special cases, the President will be authorized to grant exceptions to this stipulation.

If all the four matches in the quarterfinals cannot be arranged at the same place, the matches whose winners will have to meet in the following semifinals must—except for cases of force majeure—be arranged at the same respective places. If for reasons of force majeure two matches whose winners will have to meet in a semifinal are not arranged at the same place, this semifinal will have to follow with the shortest possible interval.

7 The match for the 3rd and 4th places shall commence as soon as possible after the termination of the semifinals.
8 The final shall commence in such time as to be terminated before the end of the calendar year.
9 *Vacancies:*
 A If one of the eight players cannot participate in the quarterfinal for which he is qualified, the vacancy is to be filled by the player who is his first substitute according to clauses 1 and 2.
 B If one of the winners of the quarterfinals cannot participate in the semifinal for which he is qualified, the player who should have played against him is to be considered as winner of the semifinal.
 C If one of the winners of the semifinals cannot participate in the final, the vacancy is to be filled by the player who has obtained the 3rd place.
10 The players in the final should as a general rule play three games a week, each round to be followed by a day devoted to unfinished games. The 7th day should be free. The players in the other matches should as a general rule play four games a week, two rounds to be followed by a day devoted to unfinished games. The 7th day should be free.

Art. 7

The match for the Men's World Championship

1 The Match for the title of Men's World Champion will take place every three years in accordance with the following regulations.
2 In the first place, it will be for the winner of the last Candidates Competition to play a match against the World Champion.
3 If the World Champion refuses to defend his title during the year designated, the new Champion will be proclaimed after a match between the two players gaining the first two prizes in the Candidates Competition.
4 If the winner of the Candidates Competition refuses to play for the title of World Champion during the year designated, the title is to be contested in a match with the Champion by the player who took the second prize in the said Candidates Competition.
5a While observing the provisions of point 12 below, the date of the match according to points 2 to 4 above is to be fixed in such a manner that the match will begin not later than July 1 in the year immediately following that in which the Candidates Competition was organized.
5b If, however, one of the two players does not appear on the date fixed according to point 5a, the procedure will be as follows:
 Ia If the said player does not submit a certificate from an official doctor attesting that his state of health

does not permit him to play, the match will be cancelled.

Ib Instead of the match thus cancelled, a match will be played as soon as possible between the other player and the player, who, according to the list of results of the Candidates Competition, is the first substitute.

IIa If, on the other hand, the said player submits a certificate as provided for in point Ia, a certain postponement, not exceeding 6 months, will be accorded to him. In the event the player's state of health at the end of this period still does not permit him to play, the match will be cancelled.

IIb Instead of the match thus cancelled, a match will be played as soon as possible between the other player and the player who, according to the list of results of the Candidates Competition, is the first substitute.

III In the event a player does not appear on the date fixed for the commencement of a match according to point Ib or point IIb, provisions analogous to those of points I or II will be applicable.

6 The World Champion will retain his title if he draws a match organized according to points 2, 4 or 5 above.

7 The national federation of the challenger has the right to organize the first twelve games of the match and the national federation of the World Champion has the right to organize the last twelve games (and the supplementary games). If the two federations agree to organize the match in another way, this ought to be accepted. However, if no agreement accepted by both players can be reached, the match is to be organized in a neutral country. The match shall be played in such time of the year when the climatic conditions in the countries concerned are most favourable, and every effort shall be made to ensure the most favourable conditions possible for the competitors.

8 The match for the World Championship will comprise 24 games. Nevertheless, when a player has gained 12½ points, he is to be declared winner, and the match will be considered as concluded.

9a Each player should as a general rule play three games a week, every round to be followed by a day devoted to unfinished games. The 7th day should be free.

9b The games will last 5 hours with time control for the execution of 40 moves in two and a half hours, the time assigned to adjourned games is 6 hours with the time control for the execution of 16 moves an hour.

10 During the period of the match every participant is entitled —but cannot be compelled—to stay away from play three times on account of ill health duly attested by an official doctor.

11 Each participant in the match is entitled to have a second who alone has the right of assisting him at the time of the

analysis. All controversial questions will be settled personally by the arbiter of the match. It is the duty of the arbiter to make sure that this regulation is strictly observed. The chief arbiter and the assistant arbiter must each belong to a neutral country and they should as far as possible consult together before making any important decision.

12 The organizing federation should communicate as soon as possible with those who will be participating in the match and, in collaboration with them, draw up a proposal regarding the place and date for the match as also the details of organization for same. The organizing federation should then submit the proposal as soon as possible to the President accompanied by a report on the opinions and wishes expressed by the players. If the proposal has received the approval of the players, the President should confine himself to indicating any modifications he considers necessary in view of FIDE provisions in force. If, on the other hand, there are differences of opinion between the organizing federation and the players or between the players themselves it is for the President to give a decision as soon as possible on the question in dispute. The decision of the President should in all cases be given at least four months before the commencement of the match. The players are entitled to address themselves directly to the President on these matters.

13 All questions not provided for in these regulations are to be settled by the Congress of the FIDE or, between Congresses, by the President.

Art. 9

Expenses

For zonal and interzonal tournaments as well as candidates competitions the travelling expenses of each participant are to be paid by his national federation, while board, lodging and pocket money during the tournament will be provided by the organizing federation. For the interzonal tournaments and the candidates competitions the travelling expenses as also the board, lodging and pocket money of the chief referee are to be paid by the organizing federation. For the matches organized according to articles 7 and 8 the travelling expenses, board, lodging and pocket money of each participant and for one person accompanying him as well as for the two referees are to be paid by the organizing federation.

Art. 10

Cash prizes

Zonal Tournaments

a At each zonal tournament prizes will be distributed to at least 50% of the participants.

b First prize shall be at least Swiss Francs 1,000.*
c Second prize shall be at least 60% of the first prize.
d Last prize shall be at least 10% of the first prize.

Interzonal Tournaments

a At each interzonal tournament prizes shall be distributed to at least 50% of the participants.
b The total amount shall be at least S. F. 12,000.
c First prize shall be at least S. F. 2,500.
d Second prize shall be at least 60% of the first prize.
e Last prize shall be at least 10% of the first prize.

Candidates matches

a	quarterfinals (winner-loser)	S. F. 1,000/600
b	semifinals (winner-loser)	S. F. 2,000/1200
c	final (winner-loser)	S. F. 3,000/1800
d	match for the 3rd/4th place (winner-loser)	S. F. 1,000/600

Match for the World Championship

Title holder	S. F. 15,000
Challenger	S. F. 9,000

All prizes to be paid in the currency of the organizing federation's country, if permission cannot be obtained to transfer the prizes in another currency which the prize-winner prefers.

Art. 11

Supplementary provisions

Any supplementary provisions are to be fixed by the President, though the General Assembly will retain its rights according to Articles 7.13 and 8.13 of these regulations.

Art. 12

General rules

1 For the tournaments referred to in these regulations, the Rules of Chess of the FIDE are to be strictly applied.
2 If in a tournament or match several players obtain the same number of points, the following rules will be applied:
A The prizes will be divided equally between these players.
B If the order of these players is decisive for the title of Men's or Ladies' World Champion, the following procedure will be observed:
B 1 If one of the players is holder of the World Championship the rule of Art. 7.6 resp. 8.6 is to be applied;
B 2 In other cases than that stated in B 1) an elimination match consisting of one or more series of supplementary games is to be organ-

* A Swiss franc is worth 28 cents.

ized, until a decision is reached. Every such series is to comprise 4 games.

C If the order of the players is decisive for the right of participating in a future match or tournament, an elimination competition is to be organized as follows:

C 1 In the candidates competitions the rules of Art. 5 and 6 are to be applied.

C 2 In the interzonal tournaments there should, if it concerns two players, be a single series comprising 6 games.

C 3 In other cases concerning two players there should be a single series comprising 4 games.

C 4 In other cases concerning more than two players there should be a single series in which each player is to meet every other player in 2 games. If a procedure according to C 2), C 3) or C 4) does not bring a decision, the order of the players will be determined according to the Sonneborn-Berger system, applied to the position of the players before the elimination competition.

D It is not necessary to take into account the defection of more than three qualified players for the application of the procedure indicated in points C 2), C 3) and C 4). The players whose admission may come into question by further vacancies will be directly classified according to the Sonneborn-Berger system.

E The Sonneborn-Berger system implies that every player is assigned a number of points calculated by a special rule for evaluation of the results, viz., that every won game is given the number of points gained in the tournament by the adversary and every drawn game is given half that number of points.

F A player who according to the preceding provisions of this article is entitled to participate in an elimination competition is at liberty to renounce that right, his case being then judged as if he came last among the players that gained the same number of points as he did.

3 Entries to any one of the tournaments and matches have to be made not later than at the date when according to the prescriptions of the Financial Regulations the entry fee must be paid to the FIDE Bureau,* viz. not later than 14 days before the commencement of the competition.

If a player who has entered for participation in a competition withdraws his entry less than 14 days before the commencement of the latter or does not put in an appearance at the commencement of the competition, and if he does

* Please note that the payments have to be effected to: „Fédération Internationale des Échecs F. I. D. E. Service „Notariat", Compte 121 12 10–1 Skandinaviska Banken Box 40085 106 40 STOCKHOLM".

not furnish acceptable reasons for his default, the entry fee is forfeited.

4 If within 30 days after the end of a competition the organizing federation informs the President that it has the intention to publish a book on it in one of the most common languages, it is the duty of the other federations to take all possible measures in order that no other books on the competition be published in the same language during the first year after the end of the competition.

Lugano, October 23, 1968.
FOLKE ROGARD
President of FIDE

REGULATIONS FOR THE ZONAL AND INTERZONAL TOURNAMENTS IN 1969 AND 1970

Art. 1

Division into Zones

For the period of 1969–1971 the zones of FIDE have been composed as follows:

Zone 1. (West-European Zone)

South Africa	Italy
Andorra	Luxemburg
England	Morocco
Belgium	Monaco
Scotland	Netherlands
Spain	Portugal
France	Switzerland
Ireland	Tunisia

Zone 2. (Central European Zone)

Federal Germany	Finland
Democratic Germany	Iceland
Austria	Norway
Denmark	Sweden

Zone 3. (East-European Zone)

Albania	Malta
Bulgaria	Poland
Cyprus	Rumania
Greece	Czechoslovakia
Hungary	Yugoslavia
Lebanon	Turkey

Zone 4. (Zone U. S. S. R.)

U. S. S. R.

Zone 5. (Zone U. S. A.)

U. S. A.

Zone 6. (Canadian Zone)

Canada

Zone 7. (Central American Zone)

Colombia
Costa Rica
Cuba
Dominican Republic
Ecuador
Mexico
Nicaragua
Panama
Puerto Rico
El Salvador
Venezuela
Virgin Islands

Remark: The local federation of the Dutch Antilles, though remaining affiliated to the Dutch Federation, will be entitled to participate with one player, respectively one woman player, in the zonal tournaments of Zone 7.

Zone 8. (South American Zone)

Argentina
Bolivia
Brazil
Chile
Paraguay
Peru
Uruguay

Zone 9. (West Asiatic Zone)

India
Iran
Israel
Mongolia

Zone 10. (East Asiatic Zone)

Australia
China
Hongkong
Indonesia
Japan
Malaya
New Zealand
Philippines
Singapore
Thailand

Art. 2

Men's Zonal Tournaments

In each zone a zonal tournament will take place in 1969 to designate the players entitled to participate in the Interzonal Tournament of 1970.

The Vice-Presidents in charge will be responsible for the general organization of these tournaments in conformity with the regulations of FIDE.

Zones 1, 2 and 3

Introductory remarks

Regarding these zones it has been considered appropriate in order to equalize the playing strength of each one of the three zonal tournaments, to admit to each one of the latter ones not only players from the zone but also players from the other zones and belonging to federations which in view of their exceptional playing strength have been judged entitled to participate in those three zonal tournaments with two or more players.

* * *

67 players will participate in the three zonal tournaments —to begin not before May 1st and not later than September 1st —in which the federations of the three zones are entitled to be represented as follows:

South Africa	by 1 player	Austria	by 2 players
Andorra	by 1 "	Denmark	by 2 "
England	by 2 "	Finland	by 2 "
Belgium	by 1 "	Iceland	by 2 "
Scotland	by 1 "	Norway	by 1 "
Spain	by 2 "	Sweden	by 2 "
France	by 1 "	Albania	by 1 "
Ireland	by 1 "	Bulgaria	by 3 "
Italy	by 1 "	Cyprus	by 1 "
Luxemburg	by 1 "	Greece	by 1 "
Morocco	by 1 "	Hungary	by 5 "
Monaco	by 1 "	Lebanon	by 1 "
Netherlands	by 3 "	Malta	by 1 "
Portugal	by 1 "	Poland	by 2 "
Switzerland	by 2 "	Rumania	by 2 "
Tunisia	by 1 "	Czechoslovakia	by 4 "
Federal Germany	by 4 "	Yugoslavia	by 6 "
Democratic Germany	by 3 "	Turkey	by 1 "
		Total	67 players

The tournaments will be composed as follows (a figure in brackets after the name of a country indicates that the place so numbered is considered by the corresponding federation to pertain to the player in question in conformity with its estimation of the mutual order of its representatives in the zonal tournaments according to their playing strength):

Zonal Tournament 1

Players from Zone 1

South Africa		1
England	(1)	1
Belgium		1
Scotland		1
Spain		2
France		1
Ireland		1
Italy		1
Luxemburg		1
Monaco		1
Netherlands	(1)	1
Portugal		1
Switzerland	(1)	1
Tunisia		1
Andorra		1
Morocco		1

Players from the other zones

Federal Germany	(2)	1
Bulgaria	(3)	1
Hungary	(3)	1
Czechoslovakia	(2)	1
Yugoslavia	(1 and 6)	2
	Total	23 players

Zonal Tournament 2

Players from Zone 2

Federal Germany	(3 and 4)	2
Democratic Germany	(1 and 3)	2
Austria	(1)	1
Denmark	(1)	1
Finland		2
Iceland	(2)	1
Norway		1
Sweden		2

Players from the other zones

Bulgaria	(2)	1
Hungary	(1 and 5)	2
Malta		1
Netherlands	(2)	1
Poland	(2)	1
Rumania	(2)	1
Czechoslovakia	(3)	1
Yugoslavia	(2 and 4)	2
	Total	22 players

Zonal Tournament 3

Players from Zone 3

Albania		1
Bulgaria	(1)	1
Cyprus		1
Greece		1
Hungary	(2 and 4)	2
Lebanon		1
Poland	(1)	1
Rumania	(1)	1
Czechoslovakia	(1 and 4)	2
Yugoslavia	(2 and 5)	2
Turkey		1

Players from the other zones

Federal Germany	(1)	1
Democratic Germany	(2)	1
England	(2)	1
Austria	(2)	1
Denmark	(2)	1
Iceland	(1)	1
Netherlands	(3)	1
Switzerland	(2)	1
	Total	22 players

The President will address to each affiliated federation a request that he be informed at the latest by December 31st, 1968 whether it intends to participate, and in this case with what number of players. If a federation does not reply to this request by December 31st, 1968 at the latest, it will have forfeited its right to participate.

Each federation intending to participate will then not later than by March 31st, 1969 send to the President a list of the players who have been chosen to take part in the tournaments. The list should give the names of a number of players exceeding by not less than three the number of players entitled to participate and the players should be listed in order of their playing strength. This list will be used for placing the players in the resp. tournaments and for filling vacancies. It must be observed

a) that only players named on the list may be admitted to a tournament and
b) that no player may play as substitute for a player placed below him on the list, so that e.g. player No. 1 may never be used as substitute for any other player.

A vacancy caused by the absence of a federation or lack of substitute will not be filled, except that in the case of a zonal tournament being organized by a federation which has the right to participate with only one player in the three tournaments this federation may fill one vacancy by one of its own players.

Should 23 players be registered for participation in Zonal Tournament 1, the President would be entitled to transfer one player to Zonal Tournament 2 or 3 in case of a vacancy in one of these tournaments.

Zone 4.

Detailed arrangements for the tournament will be made by the Federation of the U. S. S. R.

Zone 5.

Detailed arrangements for the tournament will be made by the Federation of the U. S. A.

Zone 6.

Detailed arrangements for the tournament will be made by the Canadian Federation.

Zone 7.

Detailed arrangements for the tournament will be made by the Vice-President, observing that each affiliated federation will be entitled to be represented by at least one player and by several players according to its strength in chess.

The Vice-President will address to each federation a request for information concerning the players who the federation proposes for participation and after examining the proposed names as to their playing strength he will fix the number of participants and their names. However, if the President receives objections to these decisions, he will have to decide, after having, if time permits, consulted the members of the Qualification Committee.

Zone 8.

See Zone 7.

Zone 9.

See Zone 7.

Zone 10.

See Zone 7.

Art. 4

Men's Interzonal Tournament

The Interzonal Tournament will take place in 1970 with 24 participants.

1 The 23 players who have obtained the best places in the zonal tournaments of 1969 will be entitled to participate; the number of players from each of these tournaments being fixed as follows:

Zonal	tournament	1			3 players
"	"	2			3 "
"	"	3			3 "
"	"	of zone		4	4 "
"	"	"	"	5	3 "
"	"	"	"	6	1 "
"	"	"	"	7	1 "
"	"	"	"	8	3 "
"	"	"	"	9	1 "
"	"	"	"	10	1 "

Not later than December 31st, 1969 each Vice-President in whose Zone a zonal tournament has taken place, should send to the FIDE Bureau the list of results of the tournament. The players will be entitled to participate in the Interzonal Tournament in the order of the results indicated on these lists.

If a zonal tournament has not taken place in one of the zones 4–10, the Vice-President should send to the FIDE Bureau a list of players from the zone, listed in order according to his estimate of their playing strength. This list will replace the list of the zonal tournament. However, if the President receives objections to the list, he will have to fix its composition, taking into account that it must comprise only players belonging to the zone in question. Before making his decision the President should, if time permits, consult the members of the Qualification Committee.

If a player classed on a list as qualified for the Interzonal Tournament cannot participate, the vacancy will be filled by a player from the same list in the order listed, or, if this cannot be done, by a player from the organizing federation nominated by that federation, on condition that it is not already represented in the tournament and that the player thus nominated is a grandmaster or an international master of FIDE. If the organizing federation cannot use this privilege, the vacancy will not be filled.

2 The 24th place will be given to the player who, in the preceding candidates competition, has obtained the third place or, if he cannot participate, to the player who in the said tournament obtained the fourth place; a further vacancy will not be filled.

Art. 6

General Rules

Each participant should as a general rule play only 6 games in each period of 9 days; 3 rounds should be followed by a day devoted to unfinished games, and the 9th day should be free.

Lugano, October 23, 1968.
FOLKE ROGARD
President of FIDE

Appendix B

In addition to the normal rules for the world championship competition, special rules were drawn up just for the Fischer/Spassky match. These are the special rules:

1 The match will comprise 24 games. When a player has gained 12.5 or 13 points he is to be declared the winner and the match will be considered as concluded.

2 If the position of the match after 24 games is 12–12 the reigning World Champion retains his title. In that case the prize money will be equally divided between the two players.

3 The time control is 2½ hours for the first 40 moves and for every 16 moves afterwards another hour with the accumulation of time.

4 The drawing of lots to determine colors for the first game will be carried out in the following way.

The Chief Arbiter will invite the World Champion to choose one of two envelopes containing the names of the participants.

The player whose name is chosen will have the right to choose colors from pawns held in the hands of the other player.

5 If a player is more than one hour late for the start of a game he loses that game by forfeit.

6 In principle, no postponement of games is allowed. Exceptionally, a player can postpone without penalty three playing sessions (including adjourned games) throughout the entire match because of illness or injury. The illness or injury in question must be certified to the Chief Arbiter by the Official Doctor of the match. Such certification should be given to the Arbiter not later than noon of the day of the game, except in case of a sudden illness or injury certified to by the Official Doctor. If a player must postpone a fourth session because of illness or injury, he loses that game by forfeit. Similarly, loss of game occurs with a fifth postponement and so on.

7 Games shall be played in accordance with the schedule given at the end of these rules.

8 If two games are to be continued on a day devoted to unfinished games, the game from the earliest round will be continued first. After a pause of thirty minutes following its completion, the game from the next round will be continued providing that at least two hours of playing time remains for this second game.

9 All games must be finished before the commencement of the 24th game. Likewise an adjourned game which might terminate the match—one of the participants gaining 12.5 or 13 points, or the World Champion gaining 12 points—will be finished before the next game starts.

10 The games will be played according to the FIDE Laws of Chess.

The decisions and rules of the FIDE Congresses for the present cycle are primarily relevant for the match.

11 The Chief Arbiter is grandmaster Lothar Schmid.

The Assistant Arbiter in the Icelandic part of the match is Mr. Arnlaugsson.

The Icelandic organizers will nominate an Official Doctor for their part of the match, acceptable to both parties.

12 Decisions of the Chief Arbiter are executive. Written complaints against his decisions can be lodged within, and not later than, six hours after completion of the playing session to the Tournament Committee composed of five persons: the Chief Arbiter, his assistant, one designated by the host federation with the consent of both players, and one designated by each of the players. The Committee reaches decisions within twelve hours of the lodging of a complaint and its decisions are final. If the protest is against a decision by an Arbiter, that Arbiter does not participate in the Committee vote.

A protest, as a rule, is submitted by the participant. In some cases connected with violations of this agreement which have taken place outside the playing scene or to which the participant could not react, a protest may be submitted by a second of the participant.

13 The duty of the Chief Arbiter and his assistant is to ensure a strict execution of all the conditions of this agreement and the regulations of FIDE concerning this competition. During a game at least one of the arbiters must be present on the playing scene. Decisions of the Chief Arbiter (or, in his absence, of the Assistant Arbiter) must be fulfilled.

14 The distribution of the prize money will be 62.5% to the winner and 37.5% to the loser, to each in the currency

of his choice. If after 24 games the score is 12–12 each player will receive 50%.

15 In all matters of income, the organizers guarantee that the players will receive equal rights.

16 Only the players, the arbiters and a maximum of three persons to keep score and to make moves on the demonstration board are allowed to enter the scene of play. The entrance/exit of the players is prohibited to any other persons than those allowed on the stage; their restroom and toilet is restricted to use by the players and the Arbiter during playing time.

17 In accordance with the highest principles of sportsmanship and gentlemanly conduct, each player will observe the Laws of Chess, and do his utmost not to distract or annoy his opponent, especially when the opponent is on the move.

18 The organizers of the match must provide premises for play with the best conditions of lighting, temperature, ventilation and noiselessness in accordance with the wishes of both participants.

The chess equipment for play (the table, chess board, chess pieces and the clock) is chosen for each half of the match with the permission of both participants and cannot undergo changes, an exception being made only for a defect of the clock established by the arbiter.

The participants, their seconds and the representatives of the national federations of the countries of the World Champion and the Challenger are entitled to examine in advance the premises and the chess equipment and make their remarks which should be taken into consideration by the organizers and do not contradict the wishes of the other participant.

The Chief Arbiter shall designate an area near the scene of play, out of sight and hearing of the players, where a player who desires to walk or eat may do so while his opponent is on the move.

19 During the game the participants are not allowed to accept help in any way, including the use of technical means. The participants are entitled to address only the arbiters.

Urgent medical aid to the participants during the game may be rendered only by an official doctor of the competition with the permission of the Chief Arbiter.

20 The organizers agree to strictly control the spectators and to do their utmost to assure that no noise or disturbance intrudes upon the playing area.

21 All taking of still photographs and any disturbance of the players during play is forbidden without the express permission of both players. The only filming, videotaping or televising allowed will be that which is exclusively and officially arranged by the organizers. Therefore, unless prior permission has been given by both players, no cameras will be allowed in the playing room except those required for the official uses described in the preceding sentence. The organizers guarantee that these official cameras will be neither visible nor audible to the players and they will not be disturbed in any way, such as by flash, extra lights, or extra personnel in the playing area.

22 Each participant may have one second, whose name must be known to the Chief Arbiter. The second may be replaced according to the wish of the participant, of which the Chief Arbiter must be informed.

23 The Chief Arbiter is responsible for the secrecy of the envelope with the sealed move.

24 In case of noise in or near the playing scene the Chief Arbiter is entitled, on the request of one or both of the players, to move the game temporarily to some other place, but not if either of the players has left less than 20 minutes on his clock.

25 The players shall endeavor to settle all controversial issues by agreement and in the spirit of the lofty principles of FIDE.

Games are played from 17.00 to 22.00 hours, adjourned games from 17.00 to 23.00 hours. Friday games start at 2.30. On Fridays only four hours are played for adjourned games, the times are put forward in the afternoon.

These rules are agreed upon between the Chess Federation of the U.S.S.R. (Mrs. A. Ivushkina and grandmaster E. Geller, the latter being authorized to sign for grandmaster Spassky), of the USA (Mr. E. B. Edmondson, authorized to sign for grandmaster Fischer), of Yugoslavia (Mr. P. Basaraba and Mr. M. Molerovic) and of Iceland (Mr. C. G. Thorarinsson and Mr. Fridjonsson), and approved by the President of the FIDE (Dep. President N. Rabell Mendez).

Amsterdam, March 20, 1972.